200 low-calorie recipes

200 low-calorie recipes

hamlyn **all color**

An Hachette UK Company
www.hachette.co.uk

First published in Great Britain in 2010 by Hamlyn,
a division of Octopus Publishing Group Ltd,
Endeavour House
189 Shaftesbury Avenue
London
WC2H 8JG
www.octopusbooksusa.com

Copyright © Octopus Publishing Group Ltd 2010

Distributed in the U.S. and Canada by Octopus Books USA:
c/o Hachette Book Group
237 Park Avenue
New York, NY 10017

Some of the recipes in this book have previously
appeared in other books published by Hamlyn.

ISBN: 978-0-600-62157-7

Printed and bound in China

1 2 3 4 5 6 7 8 9 10

Standard level spoon measures are used in all recipes.

Ovens should be preheated to the specified temperature—
if using a fan-assisted oven, follow the manufacturer's
instructions for adjusting the time and the temperature.

Fresh herbs and spices (including chiles) should be used
unless otherwise stated.

The Food and Drug Administration advises that eggs should
not be consumed raw. This book contains some dishes made
with raw or lightly cooked eggs. It is prudent for vulnerable
people such as pregnant and nursing mothers, invalids,
the elderly, babies, and young children to avoid uncooked or
lightly cooked dishes made with eggs. Once prepared, these
dishes should be kept refrigerated and used promptly.

This book includes dishes made with nuts and nut derivatives.
It is advisable for those with known allergic reactions to
nuts and nut derivatives and those who may be potentially
vulnerable to these allergies, such as pregnant and nursing
mothers, invalids, the elderly, babies, and children, to avoid
dishes made with nuts and nut oils. It is also prudent
to check the labels of prepared ingredients for the
possible inclusion of nut derivatives.

contents

introduction

introduction

With all the tempting food available to us at all times of the day, it is no wonder that most of us are a little overweight. For many of us, our downfall is that we simply enjoy eating good food, but it is possible to eat well and still watch the calories.

This book is designed to help those people who are trying to lose weight by offering a range of delicious recipes that are low in calories but still high in flavor. Each recipe shows a calorie count per portion, so you will know exactly what you are eating. These are recipes for real and delicious food, not ultra-dieting meals, so they will help you maintain your new healthier eating plan for life. They must be used as part of a balanced diet, with the cakes and sweet dishes eaten only as an occasional treat.

The risks of obesity

Up to half of women and two-thirds of men are overweight or obese in the developed world today. Being overweight not only can make us unhappy with our appearance, but can also lead to serious health problems, including heart disease, high blood pressure and diabetes.

When someone is obese, it means they are overweight to the point that it could start to seriously threaten their health. In fact, obesity ranks as a close second to smoking as a possible cause of cancer. Obese women are

more likely to have complications during and after pregnancy, and people who are overweight or obese are also more likely to have coronary heart disease, gallstones, osteoarthritis, high blood pressure, and type 2 diabetes. The World Health Organization (WHO) has predicted that 300 million people will have developed type 2 diabetes by 2025 due to the worldwide problem of obesity.

How can I tell if I am overweight?

The best way to tell if you are overweight is to work out your body mass index (BMI). If using U.S. standard measurements, divide

your weight in pounds (lb) by your height in inches (in) squared and multiply by 703. If using metric measurements, divide your weight in kilograms (kg) by your height in metres (m) squared. (For example, if you are 1.7 m tall and weigh 70 kg, the calculation would be 70 ÷ 2.89 = 24.2.) Then compare the figure to the list below (these figures apply only to healthy adults).

Less than 20	underweight
20–25	healthy
25–30	overweight
Over 30	obese

As we all know by now, one of the major causes of obesity is eating too many calories.

What is a calorie?

Our bodies need energy to stay alive, grow, keep warm, and be active. We get the energy we need to survive from the food and drinks we consume—more specifically, from the fat, carbohydrate, protein, and alcohol that they contain.

A calorie (cal), as anyone who has ever been on a diet will know, is the unit used to measure how much energy different foods contain. A calorie can be scientifically defined as the energy required to raise the temperature of 1 gram of water from 58°F to 60°F. A kilocalorie (kcal) is 1,000 calories and it is, in fact, kilocalories that we usually mean when we talk about the calories in different foods.

Different food types contain different numbers of calories. For example, a gram of carbohydrate (starch or sugar) provides 3.75 kcal, protein provides 4 kcal per gram, fat provides 9 kcal per gram, and alcohol provides 7 kcal per gram. So, fat is the most concentrated source of energy—weight for weight, it provides just over twice as many calories as either protein or carbohydrate— with alcohol not far behind. The energy content of a food or drink depends on how many grams of carbohydrate, fat, protein, and alcohol are present.

How many calories do we need?

The number of calories we need to consume varies from person to person, but your body weight is a clear indication of whether you are eating the right amount. Body weight is simply determined by the number of calories you are eating compared to the number of calories your body is using to maintain itself and needed for physical activity. If you regularly consume more calories than you use up, you will start to gain weight as extra energy is stored in the body as fat.

Based on our relatively inactive modern-day lifestyles, most nutritionists recommend that women should aim to consume around 2,000 calories (kcal) per day, and men an amount of around 2,500. Of course, the amount of energy required depends on your level of activity: the more active you are, the more energy you need to maintain a stable weight.

A healthier lifestyle

To maintain a healthy body weight, we need to expend as much energy as we eat; to lose weight, energy expenditure must, therefore, exceed intake of calories. So, exercise is a vital tool in the fight to lose weight. Physical activity doesn't just help us control body weight; it also helps to reduce our appetite and is known to have beneficial effects on the heart and blood that help prevent against cardiovascular disease.

Many of us claim we don't enjoy exercise and simply don't have the time to fit it into our hectic schedules. So the easiest way to increase physical activity is by incorporating it into our daily routines, perhaps by walking or cycling instead of driving (particularly for short journeys), taking up more active hobbies, such as gardening, and taking small and simple steps, such as using the stairs instead of the elevator whenever possible.

As a general guide, adults should aim to undertake at least 30 minutes of moderate-intensity exercise, such as a brisk walk, five times a week. The 30 minutes does not have to be taken all at once: three sessions of 10 minutes are equally beneficial. Children and young people should be encouraged to take at least 60 minutes of moderate-intensity exercise every day.

Some activities will use up more energy than others. The following list shows some examples of the energy a person weighing 132 lb (60 kg) would expend doing the following activities for 30 minutes:

activity	energy
Ironing	69 kcal
Cleaning	75 kcal
Walking	99 kcal
Golf	129 kcal
Fast walking	150 kcal
Cycling	180 kcal
Aerobics	195 kcal
Swimming	195 kcal
Running	300 kcal
Sprinting	405 kcal

Make changes for life

The best way to lose weight is to try to adopt healthier eating habits that you can easily maintain all the time, not just when you are trying to slim down. Aim to lose no more than 2 lb (1 kg) per week to ensure you lose only your fat stores. People who go on crash diets lose lean muscle as well as fat and are much more likely to put the weight back on again soon afterward.

For a woman, the aim is to reduce her daily calorie intake to around 1,500 kcal while she is trying to lose weight, then settle on around 2,000 per day thereafter to maintain her new body weight. Regular exercise will also make a huge difference: the more you can burn, the less you will need to diet.

Improve your diet

For most of us, simply adopting a more balanced diet will reduce our calorie intake and lead to weight loss. Follow these simple recommendations:

Eat more starchy foods, such as bread, potatoes, rice, and pasta. Assuming these replace the fattier foods you usually eat, and you don't smother them with oil or butter, this will help reduce the amount of fat and increase the amount of fiber in your diet. Try Cranberry Muffins (see page 22) or Potato Griddle Cakes (see page 34) for brunch, or Wild Rice Jambalaya (see page 108) for a satisfying supper. As a bonus, try to use whole-grain rice, pasta, and flour, because the energy from these foods is released more slowly in the body, making you feel fuller for longer.

Eat more fruit and vegetables, aiming for at least five portions of different fruit and vegetables a day (excluding potatoes).

As long as you don't add extra fat to your fruit and vegetables in the form of cream, butter, or oil, these changes will help reduce your fat intake and increase the amount of fiber and vitamins you consume. Perhaps you could start the day with the Fruity Summer Milkshake (see page 16), or have Piperade with Pastrami (see page 30) for brunch. Try the healthy but delicious Chilled Gazpacho (see page 46) or Caponata Ratatouille (see page 76) for the vibrant flavors of the Mediterranean. Who said vegetables must be dull?

Eat fewer sugary foods, such as cookies, cakes, and chocolate bars. This will also help reduce your fat intake. If you want something sweet, aim for fresh or dried fruit instead.

Reduce the amount of fat in your diet, so you consume fewer calories. Choosing low-fat versions of dairy products, such as skimmed milk and low-fat yogurt, doesn't necessarily mean your food will be tasteless, as Lean Lasagna (see page 110) demonstrates. Low-fat versions are available for most dairy products, including milk, cheese, sour cream, yogurt, and even cream and butter.

Choose lean cuts of meat, such as Canadian bacon instead of regular bacon, and chicken breasts instead of thighs. Trim all visible fat off meat before cooking and avoid frying foods—broil or roast instead. Fish is naturally low in fat and can make tempting dishes, such as Ginger Scallops with Asparagus (see page 60) or Chile & Cilantro Fish Parcels (see page 70).

Simple steps to reduce your intake

Few of us have an iron will, so when you are trying to cut down make it easier on yourself by following these steps:

• Serve small portions to start with. You may feel satisfied when you have finished, but if you are still hungry you can always go back for more.

• Once you have served up your meal, put away any leftover food before you eat. Don't put heaped serving dishes on the table as you will undoubtedly pick, even if you feel satisfied with what you have already eaten.

• Eat slowly and savor your food; then you are more likely to feel full when you have finished. If you rush a meal, you may still feel hungry afterward.

• Make an effort with your meals. Just because you are cutting down doesn't mean your meals have to be low on taste as well as calories. You will feel more satisfied with a meal you have really enjoyed and will be less likely to look for comfort in a bag of potato chips or a bar of chocolate.

• Plan your meals in advance to make sure you have all the ingredients you need. Casting around in the pantry when you are hungry is unlikely to result in a healthy, balanced meal.

• Keep healthy and interesting snacks on hand for those moments when you need something to pep you up. You don't need to succumb to a chocolate bar if there are other tempting treats available.

Important note about calorie counts

All the recipes in this book are clearly marked with the number of calories (kcal) per serving. These figures assume that you are using low-fat versions of dairy products, so be sure to use skimmed milk and low-fat yogurt. They have also been calculated using lean meat, so make sure you trim meat of all visible fat and remove the skin from chicken breasts. Don't forget to take note of the number of portions each recipe makes and divide up the quantity of food accordingly, so that you know just how many calories you are consuming.

Enjoy!

Above all, enjoy trying out the new flavors and exciting recipes that this book contains. Rather than dwelling on the thought that you are denying yourself your usual unhealthy treats, think of your new regime as a positive step toward a new you. Not only will you lose weight and feel more confident, but your health will benefit, the condition of your hair and nails will improve, and you will take on a healthy glow.

breakfasts & brunches

fruity summer milkshake

Calories per serving **89**
Makes **two 10 fl oz glasses,**
  1¼ cups each
Preparation time **2 minutes**

1 ripe **peach**, halved, pitted,
  and chopped
1 cup **strawberries**
1¼ cups **raspberries**
scant 1 cup **milk**
ice cubes

Put the peach in a blender or food processor with the strawberries and raspberries and blend to a smooth puree, scraping the mixture down from the sides of the bowl if necessary.

Add the milk and blend the ingredients again until the mixture is smooth and frothy. Pour the milkshake over the ice cubes in tall glasses.

For soy milk & mango shake, replace the peach, strawberries, and raspberries with 1 large ripe mango and the juice of 1 orange. Puree as above, then pour in scant 1 cup soy milk, blend, and serve over ice cubes as above.

maple-glazed granola with fruit

Calories per serving **246**
Serves **6**
Preparation time **20 minutes**,
  plus cooling
Cooking time **5–8 minutes**

2 tablespoons **olive oil**
2 tablespoons **maple syrup**
⅓ cup **slivered almonds**
⅓ cup **pine nuts**
½ cup **sunflower seeds**
2½ tablespoons **rolled oats**
1½ cups **plain yogurt**

Fruit salad
1 **mango**, pitted, peeled, and
  sliced
2 **kiwifruit**, peeled and sliced
small bunch of **red seedless
  grapes**, halved
grated rind and juice of **1 lime**

Heat the oil in a flameproof skillet with a metal handle, add the maple syrup and the nuts, seeds, and oats and toss together.

Transfer the pan to a preheated oven, 350°F, and cook for 5–8 minutes, stirring once and moving the brown edges to the center, until the granola mixture is evenly toasted.

Let the mixture cool, then pack it into a storage jar, seal, label, and consume within 10 days.

Make the fruit salad. Mix the fruit with the lime rind and juice, spoon the mixture into dishes, and top with spoonfuls of plain yogurt and granola.

For a berry compote, to serve with the granola instead of the fruit salad, place 1¼ cups each of raspberries, blackberries, and blueberries in a pan with the grated zest and juice of 1 lemon. Heat gently until the fruit has softened and the blueberries burst, then sweeten with honey to taste. Serve with the granola and yogurt, as above.

nutty passion fruit yogurts

Calories per serving **348**
Serves **2**
Preparation time **5 minutes**,
  plus chillng

2 **passion fruit**
1 cup **plain yogurt**
¼ cup **clear honey**
scant ½ cup toasted and
  roughly chopped **hazelnuts**
4 **clementines**, peeled and
  chopped into small pieces

Halve the passion fruit and scoop the pulp into a large bowl. Add the yogurt and mix them together gently.

Put 2 tablespoonfuls of the honey in the bottom of two narrow glasses and scatter with half of the hazelnuts. Spoon half of the yogurt over the nuts and arrange half of the clementine pieces on top of the yogurt.

Repeat the layering, reserving a few of the nuts for decoration. Scatter the nuts over the top and chill the yogurts until you are ready to serve them.

For passion fruit, coconut & strawberry yogurts, soak 2 tablespoons unsweetened dried, flaked coconut in 4 tablespoons skimmed milk for 30 minutes. Mix the passion fruit and yogurt as above, also folding in the soaked coconut. Layer as above, omitting the hazelnuts and replacing the clementines with ⅔ cup quartered strawberries.

cranberry muffins

Calories per muffin **172**
Makes **12**
Preparation time **10 minutes**
Cooking time **20 minutes**

1¼ cups **all-purpose flour**
1¼ cups **self-rising flour**
1 tablespoon **baking powder**
⅓ cup **light brown sugar**
3 pieces **preserved ginger**
  from a jar, finely chopped
generous ¾ cup **dried**
  cranberries
1 **egg**
1 cup **milk**
¼ cup **vegetable oil**

Line a 12-hole muffin pan with paper muffin liners. Sift the flours and baking powder into a large bowl. Stir in the sugar, ginger, and cranberries until evenly distributed.

Beat together the egg, milk, and oil in a separate bowl, then add the liquid to the flour mixture. Using a large metal spoon, gently stir the liquid into the flour, until only just combined. The mixture should look craggy, with specks of flour still visible.

Divide the mixture between the muffin liners, piling it up in the center. Bake in a preheated oven, 400°F, for 18–20 minutes, until well risen and golden. Transfer to a wire rack and serve while still slightly warm.

For whole-wheat apricot & orange muffins, replace the all-purpose flour with 1¼ cups whole-wheat flour. Use ¾ cup chopped dried apricots instead of the cranberries and omit the ginger. Fold the finely grated zest of 1 orange into the mixture before baking.

breakfast cereal bars

Calories per bar **156**
Makes **16**
Preparation time **10 minutes**,
   plus cooling
Cooking time **35 minutes**

7 tablespoons **butter**,
   softened
2 tablespoons **light brown
   sugar**
2 tablespoons **corn syrup**
⅔ cup **millet flakes**
⅓ cup **quinoa**
generous ⅓ cup **dried
   cherries** or **cranberries**
½ cup **golden raisins**
½ cup **sunflower seeds**
2 tablespoons **sesame seeds**
¼ cup **flaxseeds**
½ cup **unsweetened dried,
   flaked coconut**
2 **eggs**, lightly beaten

Grease an 11 x 8 inch shallow, rectangular baking pan. Beat together the butter, sugar, and syrup until creamy.

Add all the remaining ingredients and beat well until combined. Turn into the pan and level the surface with the back of a large spoon.

Bake in a preheated oven, 350°F, for 35 minutes, until deep golden. Let stand to cool in the pan.

Turn out onto a wooden board and carefully cut into 16 fingers using a serrated knife.

For tropical cereal bars, prepare the recipe as above, replacing the dried cherries or cranberries with ⅓ cup finely chopped dried pineapple and replacing the golden raisins with ½ cup dried mango.

vanilla muffins

Calories per muffin **198**
Makes **12**
Preparation time **10 minutes**,
  plus cooling
Cooking time **20 minutes**

1 **vanilla bean**
scant 1 cup **milk**
scant 2⅔ cups **self-rising flour**
1 tablespoon **baking powder**
½ cup **superfine sugar**
2 **eggs**
¼ cup **vegetable oil**
scant 1 cup **plain yogurt**
confectioners' sugar, for
  dusting

Line a 12-hole muffin pan with squares of wax paper. Split the vanilla bean lengthwise, using the tip of a sharp knife, and place in a small saucepan with scant ½ cup of the milk. Bring just to a boil, then remove from the heat and let cool slightly. Remove the vanilla bean from the pan and scoop out the seeds with a teaspoon. Stir them into the milk and discard the bean.

Sift the flour and baking powder into a large bowl, then stir in the sugar. In a separate bowl, beat together the eggs, vegetable oil, yogurt, vanilla milk, and remaining milk. Using a large metal spoon, gently stir the liquid into the flour until only just combined.

Divide the mixture between the muffin liners and bake in a preheated oven, 400°F, for about 20 minutes, until well risen and golden. Transfer to a wire rack and dust with confectioners' sugar. Serve slightly warm.

For cinnamon muffins, infuse the milk in vanilla, as above, also adding 1 cinnamon stick. Let the milk cool completely before removing the cinnamon stick and vanilla bean. Complete the recipe as above. Combine 1 tablespoon granulated sugar and 1 teaspoon ground cinnamon and lightly sprinkle over the muffins just before baking.

light "n" low pancakes

Calories per serving
(2 pancakes) **150**
Serves **4**
Preparation time **10 minutes**,
plus standing
Cooking time **20 minutes**

1 cup **whole-wheat
all-purpose flour**
1 **egg**
generous 1¼ cups **milk**
1 teaspoon **vegetable oil**,
plus a little extra for cooking

Topping ideas
chopped **fresh fruit**
chopped **apple**, **raisins**, and
ground cinnamon
cottage cheese
cream cheese
fruit spread or **preserve**

Sift the flour into a bowl. Add the bran in the sifter to the flour in the bowl.

Beat the egg, milk, and oil together, then slowly add to the flour. Stir the mixture until a smooth batter forms. Let stand for about 20 minutes, then stir again.

Heat a little oil in a nonstick skillet, or spray with an oil-water spray. When the oil is hot, add 2 tablespoons of the pancake mixture and shake the pan so that it spreads. Cook the pancake for 2 minutes, until the underside is lightly browned, then flip or turn over and cook the other side for a minute or so.

Keep the pancake warm in the oven while you cook the rest—you can stack one on top of the other as they are cooked. The mixture should make eight pancakes in all. Serve with your chosen topping.

For a strawberry & lime crush, to serve with the pancakes, blend the zest and juice of 1 lime with 1 cup cleaned strawberries and 2 teaspoons honey, until you get a coarse puree. Adjust the sweetness to taste and serve with the pancakes.

piperade with pastrami

Calories per serving **186**
Serves **6**
Preparation time **20 minutes**
Cooking time **25 minutes**

6 large **eggs**
thyme sprigs, leaves removed,
   or large pinch of **dried**
   thyme, plus extra sprigs to
   garnish
1 tablespoon **olive oil**
4 oz **pastrami**, thinly sliced
salt and **black pepper**

Sofrito
3 small, red, yellow, and/or
   green **bell peppers**
1 tablespoon **olive oil**
1 **onion**, finely chopped
2 **garlic cloves**, crushed
1 lb **tomatoes**, skinned,
   seeded, and chopped

Make the sofrito. Broil or cook the bell peppers directly in a gas flame for about 10 minutes, turning them until the skins have blistered and blackened. Rub the skins from the flesh and discard. Rinse the peppers under cold running water. Halve and seed and cut the flesh into strips.

Heat the oil in a large skillet, add the onion, and cook gently for 10 minutes, until softened and transparent. Add the garlic, tomatoes, and peppers and simmer for 5 minutes, until any juice has evaporated from the tomatoes. Set aside until ready to serve.

Beat the eggs with the thyme and salt and pepper in a bowl. Reheat the sofrito. Heat the oil in a saucepan, add the eggs, stirring until they are lightly scrambled. Stir into the reheated sofrito and spoon onto plates.

Arrange slices of pastrami around the eggs and serve immediately, garnished with a little extra thyme.

For poached-egg piperade, make the sofrito as above. Split open 3 English muffins and toast on both sides. Divide the muffins between 6 plates, then spoon over the sofrito. Poach the 6 eggs instead of scrambling them, and sit them over the muffins. Dust each egg with a tiny pinch of paprika and serve, omitting the pastrami.

corn & bacon muffins

Calories per muffin **228**
Makes **12**
Preparation time **10 minutes**,
  plus cooling
Cooking time **20 minutes**

6 **bacon slices**
1 small **red onion**, finely
  chopped
1¼ cups **frozen corn kernels**
1¼ cups **fine cornmeal**
1 cup **all-purpose flour**
2 teaspoons **baking powder**
½ cup grated **cheddar
  cheese**
scant 1 cup **milk**
2 **eggs**
3 tablespoons **vegetable oil**

Lightly oil a 12-hole muffin pan. Cut off any rind and excess fat, then finely chop the bacon and dry-fry it in a pan with the onion over a moderate heat for 3–4 minutes, until the bacon is turning crisp. Cook the corn in boiling water for 2 minutes to soften.

Put the cornmeal, flour, and baking powder in a bowl and mix together. Add the corn, cheese, bacon, and onions, and stir in.

Whisk the milk with the eggs and oil and add to the bowl. Stir gently until combined, then divide among the pan sections.

Bake in a preheated oven, 425°F, for 15–20, minutes until golden and just firm. Loosen the edges of the muffins with a knife and transfer to a wire rack to cool.

For spiced-corn & scallion muffins, omit the bacon. Prepare the recipe as above, replacing the red onion with 4 scallions, sliced thinly into rounds, and add 1 teaspoon hot paprika and 1 seeded and finely chopped red chile to the mixture before baking.

potato griddle cakes

Calories per cake **68**
Makes **12**
Preparation time **10 minutes**,
  plus cooling
Cooking time **20–25 minutes**

1 lb 2 oz large **potatoes**
1½ teaspoons **baking powder**
2 medium **eggs**
⅓ cup **milk**
vegetable oil for frying
salt and **black pepper**

Cut the potatoes into small chunks and cook in boiling, lightly salted water for 15 minutes, or until completely tender. Drain well, return to the saucepan, and mash until smooth. Let cool slightly.

Beat in the baking powder, then the eggs, milk, and a little seasoning, and continue to beat until everything is evenly combined.

Heat a little oil in a heavy skillet. Drop heaped tablespoonfuls of the mixture into the pan, spacing them slightly apart, and fry for 3–4 minutes, turning once, until golden.

Transfer to a serving plate and keep warm while frying the remainder of the potato mixture. (If broiling the potato griddle cakes, put heaped spoonfuls of the mixture on an oiled, foil-lined baking sheet and cook under a preheated broiler for 5 minutes, turning once halfway through the cooking time.) Serve warm.

For mustard-potato & green bean griddle cakes, prepare the mixture as above, adding 3 oz finely sliced, blanched green beans and 1 tablespoon whole-grain mustard before cooking.

asparagus with smoked salmon

Calories per serving **150**
Serves **6**
Preparation time **10 minutes**
Cooking time **6 minutes**

7 oz trimmed **asparagus**
3 tablespoons roughly
  chopped **hazelnuts**
4 teaspoons **olive oil**
juice of 1 **lime**
1 teaspoon **Dijon mustard**
12 **quail eggs**
8 oz **smoked salmon**
salt and **black pepper**

Steam the asparagus spears over a saucepan of boiling water for 5 minutes, until just tender.

Meanwhile, broil the nuts on a piece of foil until lightly browned. Lightly mix together the oil, lime juice, and mustard with a little salt and pepper, then stir in the hot nuts. Keep warm.

Pour water into a saucepan to a depth of 1 ½ inches and bring it to a boil. Lower the eggs into the water with a slotted spoon and cook for 1 minute. Take the pan off the heat and let the eggs stand for 1 minute. Drain the eggs, rinse with cold water, and drain again.

Tear the salmon into strips and divide it among six serving plates, folding and twisting the strips attractively. Tuck the just-cooked asparagus into the salmon, halve the quail eggs, leaving the shells on if liked, and arrange on top. Drizzle with the warm nut dressing and serve sprinkled with a little black pepper.

For asparagus with prosciutto & ricotta, steam the asparagus and make the dressing as above. Divide 18 slices prosciutto between six plates, so each has 3 slices, and spoon 2 tablespoons ricotta into the center of each plate. Arrange the asparagus around the ricotta and drizzle with the dressing. Omit the quail eggs and smoked salmon.

zucchini & stilton fritters

Calories per fritter **95**
Makes **20**
Preparation time **10 minutes**
Cooking time **10 minutes**

1 tablespoon **olive oil**
1 large **zucchini**, chopped
3 **eggs**
⅔ cup **milk**
1¼ cups **self-rising flour**,
  sifted
13 oz can **flageolet or
  cannellini beans**, drained
  and rinsed
handful of **parsley**, chopped
3 **scallions**, sliced
11 oz can **corn kernels**,
  drained
3½ oz **stilton cheese**,
  crumbled

Heat a little of the oil in a nonstick skillet, add the zucchini and fry for 3–4 minutes, until golden and tender.

Beat together the eggs, milk, and flour in a bowl, then stir in the beans, parsley, scallions, corn, stilton and the cooked zucchini.

Heat the remaining oil in a nonstick skillet and add tablespoons of the mixture to the pan. Gently flatten each fritter with the back of a fork and fry for 1–2 minutes on each, side until golden. Repeat with the remaining mixture, keeping the fritters warm in a low oven.

When all the fritters are cooked, serve with tomato salsa (see page 88).

For spinach & stilton fritters, replace the zucchini with 7 oz baby spinach. Cook in a nonstick skillet with a little oil for 1–2 minutes, until wilted. Then stir in the remaining ingredients, replacing the flageolet beans with a 13 oz can of cannellini beans, and also adding a large pinch of freshly grated nutmeg. Cook and serve as above.

olive & sundried tomato biscuits

Calories per scone **198**
Makes **8**
Preparation time **15 minutes**,
  plus cooling
Cooking time **12 minutes**

1 cup **rice flour**
⅔ cup **potato flour**
1 teaspoon **xanthan gum**
1 teaspoon **baking powder**
1 teaspoon **baking soda**
6 tablespoons **butter**, cubed
2½ tablespoons chopped
  pitted green olives
4 **sundried tomatoes**,
  chopped
1 tablespoon chopped
  parsley
1 large **egg**, beaten
¼ cup **buttermilk**, plus a little
  extra for brushing

Place the flours, xanthan gum, baking powder, baking soda, and butter in a food processor and blend until the mixture resembles fine breadcrumbs, or rub in by hand in a large bowl.

Stir the olives, tomatoes, and parsley into the mixture, then, using the blade of a knife, stir in the egg and buttermilk until the mixture comes together.

Turn the dough out onto a surface dusted lightly with flour and gently press it down to a thickness of 1 inch. Use a 2 inch cutter to cut out the biscuits.

Place on a lightly floured baking sheet, brush with a little buttermilk, and place in a preheated oven, 425°F, for about 12 minutes, until golden and risen. Remove the biscuits from the oven and transfer to a wire rack to cool.

For ham & cheese biscuits, prepare the mixture as above, replacing the green olives with 1 oz roughly chopped honey-roast ham. Add 2 tablespoons freshly grated Parmesan cheese to the mixture before working in the egg and buttermilk.

light lunches

lentil & pea soup

Calories per serving **141**
Serves **4**
Preparation time **10 minutes**
Cooking time **2 hours**

1 teaspoon **olive oil**
1 **leek**, finely sliced
1 **garlic clove**, crushed
13 oz can **French green lentils**, drained
2 tablespoons chopped **mixed herbs**, such as thyme and parsley
1½ cups **frozen peas**
2 tablespoons **crème fraîche** or **sour cream**
1 tablespoon chopped **mint**
pepper

Vegetable stock
1 tablespoon **olive oil**
1 **onion**, chopped
1 **carrot**, chopped
4 **celery sticks**, chopped
any **vegetable trimmings**, such as celery tops, onion skins, and tomato skins
1 **bouquet garni**
5¼ cups **water**
salt and **black pepper**

To make the stock, heat the oil in a large saucepan, add the vegetables, and fry for 2–3 minutes, then add the vegetable trimmings and bouquet garni and season well. Pour over the water, bring to a boil and simmer gently for 1½ hours, by which time the stock should have reduced to 3½ cups. Drain over a bowl, discarding the vegetables and retaining the stock.

Heat the oil in a medium saucepan, add the leek and garlic, and fry over a gentle heat for 5–6 minutes, until the leek is softened.

Add the lentils, stock, and herbs, bring to a boil, and simmer for 10 minutes. Add the peas and continue to cook for 5 minutes.

Transfer half the soup to a liquidizer or food processor and blend until smooth. Return to the pan, stir to combine with the unblended soup, then heat through and season with plenty of pepper.

Stir together the crème fraîche and mint and serve on top of each bowl of soup.

For ham & lentil soup, to serve as a more substantial meal, add a 7 oz piece of cooked ham to the soup when adding the stock. Cook as above, but before liquidizing the soup roughly shred the ham. Blend half the ham with half the soup, then return to the pan as above. Stir in the remaining shredded ham, heat through, and complete the recipe as above.

chilled gazpacho

Calories per serving **135**
Serves **6**
Preparation time **20 minutes**,
    plus chilling

1¾ lb **tomatoes**, skinned and
    roughly chopped
½ **cucumber**, roughly
    chopped
2 **red bell peppers**, seeded
    and roughly chopped
1 **celery** stick, chopped
2 **garlic cloves**, chopped
½ **red chile**, seeded and
    sliced
small handful of **cilantro** or
    flat-leaf parsley, plus extra
    to garnish
2 tablespoons **white wine
    vinegar**
2 tablespoons **sundried
    tomato paste**
4 tablespoons **olive oil**
salt

To serve
ice cubes
hard-boiled egg, finely
    chopped
a little **cucumber, bell pepper,
    and onion**, finely chopped

Mix together the vegetables, garlic, chile, and cilantro in a large bowl.

Add the vinegar, tomato paste, oil, and a little salt. Process in batches in a food processor or blender until smooth, scraping the mixture down from the sides of the bowl if necessary.

Collect the blended mixtures together in a clean bowl and check the seasoning, adding a little more salt if needed. Chill for up to 24 hours before serving.

To serve, ladle the gazpacho into large bowls, scatter with ice cubes, and garnish with chopped parsley or cilantro and a little chopped hard-boiled egg, cucumber, bell pepper and onion, if you like.

For chilled couscous gazpacho, prepare the soup as above, omitting the red bell peppers, and chill. Place ¼ cup couscous in a bowl and pour in just enough boiling water to come ½ in above the level of the couscous. Cover with plastic wrap and set aside for 10 minutes. Uncover, break the couscous up with a fork, and let cool to room temperature. Stir into the soup just before serving with the chopped herbs and a little harissa on the side. Omit the ice and garnishes.

sweet potato & cabbage soup

Calories per serving **160**
Serves **4**
Preparation time **15 minutes**
Cooking time **25 minutes**

2 **onions**, chopped
2 **garlic cloves**, sliced
4 lean **Canadian bacon slices**, chopped
3¾ cups chopped **sweet potatoes**
2 **parsnips**, chopped
1 teaspoon chopped **thyme**
3½ cups **Vegetable Stock** (see page 44)
1 **baby savoy cabbage**, shredded

Place the onions, garlic, and bacon in a large saucepan and fry for 2–3 minutes.

Add the sweet potatoes, parsnips, thyme and stock, bring to a boil, and simmer for 15 minutes.

Transfer two-thirds of the soup to a liquidizer or food processor and blend until smooth. Return to the pan, add the cabbage, and continue to simmer for 5–7 minutes, until the cabbage is just cooked. Serve with Irish soda bread.

For squash & broccoli soup, follow the recipe as above, replacing the sweet potatoes with 3 ½ cups peeled and chopped butternut squash. After returning the blended soup to the pan, add scant 1 ½ cups small broccoli florets. Cook as above, omitting the cabbage.

bacon & white bean soup

Calories per serving **136**
Serves **4**
Preparation time **5 minutes**
Cooking time **15 minutes**

1 teaspoon **olive oil**
2 **smoked bacon slices**,
   chopped
2 **garlic cloves**, crushed
1 **onion**, chopped
a few sprigs of **thyme** or
   lemon thyme
two 13 oz cans **cannellini
   beans**, drained and rinsed
3½ cups **Vegetable Stock**
   (see page 44)
2 tablespoons chopped
   parsley
black pepper

Heat the oil in a large saucepan, then add the bacon, garlic, and onion and fry for 3–4 minutes, until the bacon is beginning to brown and the onion to soften.

Add the thyme and continue to fry for 1 minute. Then add the beans and stock to the pan, bring to a boil, and simmer for 10 minutes.

Transfer the soup to a liquidizer or food processor and blend with the parsley and pepper until smooth.

Return to the pan, heat through, and serve with fresh bread.

For herbed crostini, to serve with the soup, combine 2 tablespoons each finely chopped basil and parsley and stir into a bowl with 1 crushed garlic clove, a pinch of crushed chiles, and 1 tablespoon extravirgin olive oil. Toast 8 thin slices of baguette and brush with the herb topping just before serving.

miso broth with shrimp

Calories per serving **57**
Serves **6**
Preparation time **10 minutes**
Cooking time **7–8 minutes**

4 **scallions** or **baby leeks**,
  thinly sliced
¾ inch piece **fresh ginger**
  root, finely chopped
½–1 large **red chile**, seeded
  and thinly sliced (to taste)
6 cups **fish** or **Vegetable**
  Stock (see page 44)
3 tablespoons **chilled miso**
2 tablespoons **mirin**
  (Japanese cooking wine)
1 tablespoon **soy sauce**
scant 1½ cups thinly sliced
  bok choy
2 tablespoons chopped
  cilantro
5 oz **frozen cooked shrimp**,
  thawed and rinsed

Put the white parts of the scallions or leeks into a
saucepan with the ginger, sliced chile, and stock.

Add the miso, mirin, and soy sauce, stir, bring to a boil,
and simmer for 5 minutes.

Stir in the green parts of the scallions or leeks, the bok
choy, cilantro, and shrimp and cook for 2–3 minutes
or until the bok choy has just wilted. Ladle into bowls
and serve.

For vegetarian miso broth, prepare the soup as
above. When adding the bok choy, also stir in 1 large
carrot, cut into matchsticks, and ½ cup bean sprouts.
Cook as above for 2–3 minutes. Omit the shrimp.

sautéed kidneys with marsala

Calories per serving **303**
Serves **6**
Preparation time **20 minutes**
Cooking time **20–23 minutes**

2 tablespoons **butter**
1 tablespoon **olive oil**
1 **onion**, thinly sliced
10 **lambs' kidneys**, cored and
   trimmed
2½ cups halved **cherry
   tomatoes**
1 teaspoon **Dijon mustard**
1 teaspoon **tomato paste**
scant 1 cup **marsala**
8 **bacon slices**
2½ cups **arugula**
4 teaspoons **balsamic
   vinegar**
3 slices **whole-grain bread**
salt and **black pepper**

Heat the butter and oil in a skillet, add the onion, and cook for 5 minutes, until softened and lightly browned. Add the kidneys and fry over a high heat for 3 minutes, until browned.

Add the tomatoes and cook for 2 minutes, then stir in the mustard, tomato paste, marsala, and salt and pepper. Cook for 2–3 minutes, stirring, until the sauce has reduced slightly and the kidneys are cooked. Cover with a lid and keep hot.

Wind the bacon around eight metal skewers and broil for 8–10 minutes, until crisp. Toss the arugula in the vinegar. Toast the bread and cut each slice in half.

Arrange the toast on serving plates, reheat the kidneys if necessary, and spoon them on to the toast. Slide the skewers from the bacon and arrange the bacon attractively on the kidneys. Spoon the arugula salad on the side and serve immediately.

For beef strips with Marsala, replace the kidneys with 1 lb lean beef steak, cut into thin strips. Cook the beef with the ingredients up to and including the marsala as above, then remove from the heat and stir in thearugula, balsamic vinegar and ⅓ cup toasted pine nuts. Set aside for the arugula to wilt. Omit the bacon and toast, and serve.

peppered beef with salad greens

Calories per serving **148**
Serves **6**
Preparation time **20 minutes**
Cooking time **3–5 minutes**

2 **thick-cut sirloin steaks**,
  about 1 lb in total
3 teaspoons **colored
  peppercorns**, coarsely
  crushed
coarse salt flakes
generous ¾ cup **plain yogurt**
1–1½ teaspoons **horseradish
  sauce** (to taste)
1 **garlic clove**, crushed
5 oz **mixed salad greens**
1½ cups sliced **button
  mushrooms**
1 **red onion**, thinly sliced
1 tablespoon **olive oil**
salt and **black pepper**

Trim the fat from the steaks and rub the meat with the crushed peppercorns and salt flakes.

Mix together the yogurt, horseradish sauce, and garlic and season with salt and pepper to taste. Add the salad greens, mushrooms, and most of the red onion and toss gently.

Heat the oil in a skillet, add the steaks, and cook over a high heat for 2 minutes, until browned. Turn over and cook for 2 minutes for medium rare, 3–4 minutes for medium, or 5 minutes for well done.

Spoon the salad greens into the center of six serving plates. Thinly slice the steaks and arrange the pieces on top, then garnish with the remaining red onion.

For lemon beef with mustard dressing, trim the steaks and season with salt and a light grinding of black pepper. Make the salad as above, replacing the yogurt with ¾ cup crème fraîche or sour cream and using 2 tablespoons whole-grain mustard instead of the horseradish. Cook the steaks as above, adding the juice of ½ lemon to the skillet after removing the steaks from the heat. Turn the steaks in the lemon a couple of times, then serve as above.

chicken burgers & tomato salsa

Calories per serving **135**
Serves **4**
Preparation time **15 minutes**,
  plus chilling
Cooking time **10 minutes**

1 **garlic clove**, crushed
3 **scallions**, finely sliced
1 tablespoon **pesto**
2 tablespoons chopped
  mixed herbs, such as
  parsley, tarragon and thyme
12 oz **ground chicken**
2 **sundried tomatoes**, finely
  chopped
1 teaspoon **olive oil**

Tomato salsa
1⅔ cups quartered **cherry
  tomatoes**
1 **red chile**, seeded and finely
  chopped
1 tablespoon chopped
  cilantro
grated rind and juice of **1 lime**

Mix together all the burger ingredients, except the oil.
Divide the mixture into four and form into burgers.
Cover and chill for 30 minutes.

Combine all the salsa ingredients in a bowl.

Brush the burgers with the oil and cook under a high
broiler or on a barbecue for about 3–4 minutes each
side, until cooked through.

Serve each burger in a bread roll with the tomato salsa
and salad greens.

For lamb burgers with mint & yogurt sauce, make
the burgers as above, replacing the ground chicken
with 12 oz lean ground lamb. Instead of the salsa,
make a sauce by combining 5 tablespoons plain
yogurt, 1 red chile, seeded and finely chopped,
1 tablespoon roughly chopped mint, and a large
pinch of ground cumin.

ginger scallops with asparagus

Calories per serving **248**
Serves **4**
Preparation time **10 minutes**,
   plus marinating
Cooking time **10 minutes**

12 fresh **scallops**
2 **scallions**, thinly sliced
finely grated rind of 1 **lime**
1 tablespoon **ginger syrup**
2 tablespoons **extravirgin
   olive oil**, plus extra for
   drizzling
8 oz thin **asparagus spears**
juice of ½ **lime**
mixed salad greens
salt and **black pepper**
chervil sprigs, to garnish

Wash the scallops and pat dry. Cut each one in half
and place the pieces in a bowl.

Mix together the scallions, lime rind, ginger syrup, and
half the oil. Season to taste and pour this dressing over
the scallops. Set aside to marinate for 15 minutes.

Meanwhile, steam the asparagus spears for
5–8 minutes, until tender. Toss them with the remaining
oil and the lime juice. Season to taste and keep warm.

Heat a large, nonstick skillet until hot, add the scallops,
and fry for 1 minute on each side, until golden and just
cooked through. Add the marinade juices.

Arrange the asparagus spears, salad greens, and
chervil sprigs on plates with the scallops and any pan
juices and serve.

For scallops with prosciutto, wash and cut the
scallops, then marinate in 2 crushed garlic cloves, the
lime rind, and all the oil, omitting the scallions and
ginger syrup. Meanwhile broil 6 prosciutto slices
under a hot broiler for 2–3 minutes, until golden and
crisp. Let cool, then break the prosciutto into large
pieces. Cook the scallops as above and serve with
the prosciutto and remaining ingredients. Omit the
asparagus.

crab & cilantro cakes

Calories per serving **185**
Serves **6**
Preparation time **25–30 minutes**
Cooking time **10 minutes**

12 oz **canned crabmeat**, drained
1¼ cups **cold mashed potatoes**
2 tablespoons chopped **cilantro**
1 bunch of **scallions**, finely sliced
grated rind and juice of ½ **lemon**
2 **eggs**, beaten
flour, for coating
3 cups **fresh white bread crumbs**
1 tablespoon **oil**

Mix together, in a large bowl, the crabmeat, mashed potatoes, cilantro, scallions, lemon rind and juice, and half the beaten egg to bind.

Form the mixture into 12 cakes about ½ inch thick. Coat the cakes with flour, then dip into the remaining egg and then the bread crumbs.

Heat the oil in a nonstick skillet and fry the cakes for about 10 minutes, until golden, turning once or twice.

Drain on paper towels before serving. Serve with a sweet red chili sauce, or tomato salsa (see page 88).

For salmon & dill cakes, prepare the fish cakes as above, replacing the crab with 12 oz canned salmon and the cilantro with 2 tablespoons chopped dill. Add 2 tablespoons chopped capers to the mix before shaping, coating, and frying as above. Serve with sour cream.

parsley & garlic sardines

Calories per serving **180**
Serves **6**
Preparation time **10 minutes**,
  plus chilling (optional)
Cooking time **5 minutes**

12 **fresh sardines**, cleaned, or
  use fillets if preferred

Marinade
generous ¾ cup chopped
  parsley
1 teaspoon freshly ground
  black pepper
1 **garlic clove**, crushed
finely grated rind and juice of
  1 **lemon**
2 tablespoons **white wine**
1 tablespoon **olive oil**

Put all the ingredients for the marinade in a small saucepan. Bring to a boil, then remove from the heat.

Place the sardines on a prepared barbecue or on a preheated hot griddle or under a hot broiler. Cook for 1–2 minutes on each side, until crisp and golden.

Arrange the sardines in a single layer in a shallow dish. Pour the dressing over the sardines and serve hot. Alternatively, cover and refrigerate for at least 1 hour before serving cold, with tabbouleh and a mixed green salad, if liked.

For harissa & almond sardines, combine the ingredients for the marinade in a bowl, replacing the white wine with 1½ teaspoons harissa paste. Cook the sardines as above, arrange in a shallow dish, then spoon over the prepared marinade. Cover and refrigerate for at least 1 hour, occasionally turning the sardines in the marinade. Scatter with 2 tablespoons slivered, toasted almonds and serve as above.

lettuce wrappers with crab

Calories per serving **50**
Serves **4**
Preparation time **30 minutes**

1 **fresh cooked crab**, about
  1 lb, cleaned
4 small **iceberg lettuce
  leaves**
salt and **black pepper**

Cucumber relish
¼ **cucumber**, finely diced
3 **scallions**, thinly sliced
½ large **red chile**, seeded and
  finely chopped
2 tablespoons **white wine
  vinegar**
1 teaspoon **light soy sauce**
1 teaspoon **superfine sugar**
4 teaspoons finely chopped
  mint or **cilantro**

Make the relish by mixing all the ingredients in a bowl
with a little salt and pepper.

Twist and remove the two large claws and spiderlike
legs from the crab and set aside. With the crab upside
down, pull away the ball-like, spongy lungs. Check that
the small sac and any green matter have been
removed, then scoop the brown meat and skin from
under the shell onto a plate. Break up the crabmeat
with a spoon.

Put the crab claws into a plastic bag and hit once
or twice with a rolling pin to break the shells. Then,
working on one claw at a time, peel away the shell,
removing the white flesh with a small knife and a
skewer. Add to the brown crabmeat.

When ready to serve, spoon the crab into the lettuce
leaves and top with spoonfuls of the cucumber relish.
Roll up and eat with your fingers.

For lettuce wrappers with seared beef, make the
relish as above. Omit the crab and marinate a 10 oz
sirloin steak in 1 tablespoon Thai red curry paste for
30 minutes. Heat 2 teaspoons peanut oil in a nonstick
skillet. Brush the marinade off the steak and fry it for
1 minute on each side, until browned, then thinly slice.
Toss the beef into the relish and serve spooned into
lettuce leaves.

jumbo shrimp with pancetta

Calories per serving **187**
Serves **4**
Preparation time **5 minutes**
Cooking time **10 minutes**

1 teaspoon **olive oil**
1 tablespoon **unsalted butter**
2 oz **pancetta** or **smoked
  bacon**, finely chopped
1 lb **peeled jumbo shrimp**
grated rind and juice of
  1 **lemon**
1 large bunch of **watercress**

Heat the oil and butter in a large skillet, add the pancetta or smoked bacon, and fry for 3–4 minutes, until crisp.

Add the shrimp and fry for 1 minute on each side. Sprinkle over the lemon rind and juice and continue to fry for 1 minute, then add the watercress and combine well.

Serve as a small lunch or with potatoes or pasta as a larger main course.

For jumbo shrimp & chorizo with arugula, omit the olive oil, butter, and pancetta. Finely slice 2 oz chorizo and dry-fry in a large nonstick skillet over a low heat until crispy and some of its juices have been released. Increase the heat to high, toss in the shrimp, and complete the recipe as above, replacing the watercress with 5 cups arugula.

chile & cilantro fish parcels

Calories per serving **127**
Serves **1**
Preparation time **15 minutes**,
  plus marinating and chilling
Cooking time **15 minutes**

4 oz **cod, haddock** or **other
  white fish fillet**
2 teaspoons **lemon juice**
1 tablespoon **fresh cilantro
  leaves**
1 **garlic clove**
1 **green chile**, seeded and
  chopped
¼ teaspoon **sugar**
2 teaspoons **plain yogurt**

Place the fish in a nonmetallic dish and sprinkle with
the lemon juice. Cover and let stand in the refrigerator
to marinate for 15–20 minutes.

Put the cilantro, garlic, and chile in a food processor or
blender and process until the mixture forms a paste.
Add the sugar and yogurt and briefly process to blend.

Lay the fish on a sheet of foil. Coat the fish on both
sides with the paste. Gather up the foil loosely and turn
over at the top to seal. Return to the refrigerator for at
least 1 hour.

Place the parcel on a baking sheet and bake in a
preheated oven, 400°F, for about 15 minutes, until the
fish is just cooked.

For scallion & ginger fish parcels, place the fish
fillet on a sheet of foil. Omit the above marinade.
Combine 1 teaspoon chopped ginger and 2 thinly
sliced scallions with a pinch of superfine sugar and
the juice and rind of ½ lime. Rub the mixture all over
the fish, then seal and marinate the parcel as above
for 30 minutes. Bake as above.

crab & noodle asian wraps

Calories per serving **199**
Serves **4**
Preparation time **15 minutes**,
  plus standing
Cooking time **5 minutes**

7 oz **rice noodles**
1 bunch **scallions**, finely
  sliced
¾ inch piece **fresh ginger
  root**, grated
1 **garlic clove**, finely sliced
1 **red chile**, finely chopped
2 tablespoons chopped
  cilantro
1 tablespoon chopped **mint**
¼ **cucumber**, cut into fine
  matchsticks
two 6 oz cans **crabmeat**,
  drained, or 10 oz **fresh
  white crabmeat**
1 tablespoon **sesame oil**
1 tablespoon **sweet chili
  sauce**
1 teaspoon **Thai fish sauce**
16 **Chinese pancakes** or
  **Vietnamese rice-paper
  wrappers**

Cook the rice noodles according to the package instructions. Drain, then refresh under cold running water.

Mix together all the other ingredients, except the pancakes or rice-paper wrappers, in a large bowl. Add the noodles and toss to mix. Cover and set aside for 10 minutes to let the flavors develop, then transfer to a serving dish.

To serve, let people take a pancake or rice-paper wrapper, top with some of the crab and noodle mixture, roll up, and enjoy.

For shrimp & peanut wraps, make the mixture as above, replacing the crab with 7 oz small cooked shrimp and also adding 2 tablespoons chopped peanuts. Stir in the juice of 1 lime and wrap as above.

red pepper & feta rolls with olives

Calories per serving **146**
Serves **4**
Preparation time **10 minutes**,
  plus cooling
Cooking time **10 minutes**

2 **red bell peppers**, cored,
  seeded, and quartered
  lengthwise
3½ oz **feta cheese**, thinly
  sliced or crumbled
16 **basil leaves**
16 **black olives**, pitted and
  halved
2 tablespoons **pine nuts**,
  toasted
1 tablespoon **pesto**
1 tablespoon **fat-free French
  dressing**

Place the bell peppers skinside up on a baking sheet under a high broiler and cook for 7–8 minutes, until the skins are blackened. Remove the bell peppers and place them in a plastic bag. Fold over the top to seal and let cool for 20 minutes, then remove the skins.

Lay the skinned bell pepper quarters on a board and layer up the feta, basil leaves, olives, and pine nuts on each one.

Carefully roll up the bell peppers and secure with a toothpick. Place two bell pepper rolls on each serving plate.

Whisk together the pesto and French dressing in a small bowl and drizzle over the bell pepper rolls. Serve with arugula and some crusty bread to mop up the juices.

For red pepper, ricotta & sundried tomato rolls, broil and skin the bell peppers as above. Mix 5 chopped sundried tomatoes into 3½ oz ricotta cheese, also stirring in the basil and pine nuts. Omit the feta and black olives. Season with salt and pepper and use to top the bell pepper quarters. Roll up and serve as above.

caponata ratatouille

Calories per serving **90**
Serves **6**
Preparation time **20 minutes**
Cooking time **40 minutes**

1½ lb **eggplants**
1 large **onion**
1 tablespoon **olive oil**
3 **celery sticks**, coarsely
   chopped
a little **wine** (optional)
2 large **beef tomatoes**,
   skinned and seeded
1 teaspoon chopped **thyme**
¼–½ teaspoon **cayenne**
   pepper
2 tablespoons **capers**
handful of **pitted green olives**
¼ cup **white wine vinegar**
1 tablespoon **sugar**
1–2 tablespoons
   unsweetened **cocoa**
   (optional)
freshly ground **black pepper**

To garnish
toasted, chopped **almonds**
chopped **parsley**

Cut the eggplants and onion into ½ inch chunks.

Heat the oil in a nonstick skillet until very hot, add the eggplant and fry for about 15 minutes, until very soft. Add a little boiling water to prevent sticking if necessary.

Meanwhile, place the onion and celery in a saucepan with a little water or wine. Cook for 5 minutes, until tender but still firm.

Add the tomatoes, thyme, cayenne pepper, and eggplant and onions. Cook for 15 minutes, stirring occasionally. Add the capers, olives, wine vinegar, sugar, and cocoa (if using) and cook for 2–3 minutes.

Season with pepper and serve garnished with almonds and parsley. Serve hot or cold as a side dish, appetizer, or a main dish, with polenta and hot crusty bread, if liked.

For red pepper & potato caponata, omit the eggplants, thyme, and cocoa. Broil and skin 2 red and 2 yellow bell peppers, following the method on page 74. Cook the onions and celery as above, then follow the remainder of the recipe, adding the skinned bell peppers and 1 lb new potatoes cooked and halved, instead of the eggplants.

zucchini frittatas with mint

Calories per serving **200**
Serves **6**
Preparation time **10 minutes**
Cooking time **about 30 minutes**

1 tablespoon **olive oil**
1 **onion**, finely chopped
2 **zucchini**, about 12 oz in
  total, halved lengthwise and
  thinly sliced
6 **eggs**
1¼ cups **milk**
3 tablespoons grated
  Parmesan cheese
2 tablespoons chopped **mint**,
  plus extra leaves to garnish
  (optional)
salt and **black pepper**

Tomato sauce
1 tablespoon **olive oil**
1 **onion**, finely chopped
1–2 **garlic cloves**, crushed
  (optional)
1 lb **plum tomatoes**, chopped

Make the sauce. Heat the oil in a saucepan, stir in the onion, and fry for 5 minutes, stirring occasionally until softened and just beginning to brown. Add the garlic, if using, the tomatoes, and season with salt and pepper. Stir and simmer for 5 minutes, until the tomatoes are soft. Puree in a liquidizer or food processor until smooth, strain into a bowl and keep warm.

Heat the oil in a skillet, add the onion, and fry until softened and just beginning to brown. Add the zucchini, stir to combine, and cook for 3–4 minutes, until softened but not browned.

Beat together the eggs, milk, Parmesan, and mint, then stir in the zucchini. Season well and pour the mixture in the 12 greased sections of a deep muffin pan. Bake into a preheated oven, 375°F, for about 15 minutes, until they are lightly browned and well risen and the egg mixture has set.

Let stand in the pan for 1–2 minutes, then loosen the edges with a knife. Turn out and arrange on plates with the warm tomato sauce. Garnish with extra mint leaves, if liked.

For garlicky arugula frittatas, make the tomato sauce to serve as above. For the frittatas, omit the zucchini. Soften the onions as above, then add 2 crushed garlic cloves, stir for 1 minute, and remove from the heat. Beat together the eggs, milk, and Parmesan, as above, replacing the mint with 3¾ cups roughly chopped arugula. Add the cooked onions and bake as above.

goat cheese & herb soufflés

Calories per soufflé **277**
Serves **4**
Preparation time **10 minutes**
Cooking time **15 minutes**

2 tablespoons
  polyunsaturated margarine
6 tablespoons **all-purpose**
  flour
1¼ cups **milk**
4 **eggs**, separated
3½ oz **goat cheese**, crumbled
1 tablespoon chopped **mixed**
  herbs, such as parsley,
  chives, and thyme
1 tablespoon freshly grated
  Parmesan cheese
3¾ cups **arugula**
2 tablespoons **fat-free salad**
  dressing
salt and **black pepper**

Melt the margarine in a medium saucepan, add the flour, and cook, stirring, for 1 minute. Gradually add the milk, whisking all the time, and cook for 2 minutes, until thickened.

Remove the pan from the heat. Beat in the egg yolks one at a time, then stir in the goat cheese. Season well.

Whisk the egg whites in a large bowl until they form firm peaks, then gradually fold them into the cheese mixture with the herbs. Transfer to four lightly oiled ramekins, sprinkle over the Parmesan, then bake in a preheated oven, 375°F, for 10–12 minutes, until risen and golden.

Toss together the arugula and dressing and serve with the soufflés.

For Gruyère & mustard soufflé, cook the flour in the margarine as above, stirring in 2 teaspoons English mustard powder. Complete the recipe as above, replacing the goat cheese with ⅔ cup grated Gruyère, and omitting the Parmesan.

roasted peppers with tapenade

Calories per serving **332**
Serves **4**
Preparation time **20 minutes**
Cooking time **45 minutes**

4 **red bell peppers**, halved
  and seeded
3 tablespoons **extravirgin
  olive oil**
¾ cup **pitted black olives**
2 **garlic cloves**, roughly
  chopped
1 tablespoon chopped
  oregano
4 tablespoons **sundried
  tomato paste**
8 oz **tofu**
1⅓ cups halved **cherry
  tomatoes**
chopped **parsley**, to serve
salt and **black pepper**

Put the bell peppers, cut side up, in a roasting pan, drizzle with 1 tablespoon of the oil, and season with salt and pepper. Roast in a preheated oven, 400°F, for 25–30 minutes, until lightly browned.

To make the tapenade, put the olives, garlic, oregano, tomato paste, and the remaining olive oil in a food processor or blender. Blend to a thick paste, scraping down the mixture from the sides of the bowl.

Pat the tofu dry on paper towels and cut into ½ inch dice. Toss in a bowl with the tapenade. Pile the mixture into the bell peppers with the cherry tomatoes, and return to the oven for an additional 15 minutes, until the tomatoes have softened and the filling is hot.

Transfer to serving plates and scatter liberally with plenty of chopped fresh parsley.

For roasted bell peppers with anchovies & mozzarella, roast the halved red bell peppers for 25–30 minutes, as above. Make the tapenade, omitting the sundried tomato paste, then stir in 5 oz mini mozzarellas. Fill the bell peppers with the tapenade, cherry tomatoes, then add 2 anchovy fillets to each bell pepper. Omit the tofu. Cook and serve as above.

chile & melon sorbet with ham

Calories per serving **125**
Serves **6**
Preparation time **35 minutes**,
  plus freezing

1½ **muskmelons**, quartered
  and seeded
12 slices **Serrano ham**,
  Prosciutto crudo, or **Parma
  ham**

Sorbet
1 **muskmelon**, halved, peeled
  and seeded
2 tablespoons chopped **mint**
½–1 large **red chile**, seeded
  and finely chopped (to
  taste), plus strips of chile to
  decorate
1 **egg white**

Make the sorbet. Scoop the melon flesh into a food
processor or liquidizer and blend until smooth. Stir in
the mint and add chile to taste.

Transfer the mixture to an ice cream maker and churn
until thick. Alternatively, pour the mixture into a plastic
box and freeze for 4 hours, beating once or twice to
break up the ice crystals.

Mix in the egg white and continue churning until the
sorbet is thick enough to scoop. If you are not serving
it immediately, transfer the sorbet to a plastic box and
store in the freezer. Otherwise, freeze for a minimum
of 2 hours, until firm.

Arrange the melon quarters and ham on six serving
plates. Use warm spoons to scoop out the sorbet and
put two spoonfuls of sorbet on top of each melon
quarter. Decorate with strips of chile and serve
immediately.

For honeyed peaches, to serve with the ham
instead of the sorbet and melon quarters, make a
dressing using 1 tablespoon extravirgin olive oil,
2 tablespoons chopped mint, ½ red chile, seeded
and finely chopped, and 1 teaspoon honey. Cut
5 peaches into wedges and stir into the dressing.
Let stand to marinate for 30 minutes, then serve with
the ham slices.

red pepper rouille & vegetables

Calories per serving **154**
Serves **6**
Preparation time **30 minutes**,
  plus cooling
Cooking time **30–35 minutes**

¼ cup **olive oil**
2–3 **garlic cloves**, finely
  chopped
3 large pinches of **saffron
  threads**
3 mixed **red** and **orange bell
  peppers**, cored, seeded,
  and each cut into 6 strips
3 **zucchini**, about 1¼ oz each
2 **onions**, cut into wedges
salt and **black pepper**

Rouille
4 **plum tomatoes** about 8 oz
  total
1 **red bell pepper**, cored,
  seeded, and quartered
1 **garlic clove**, finely chopped
large pinch of **ground
  pimenton (smoked
  paprika)**
1 tablespoon **olive oil**

Put the oil for the vegetables in a large plastic bag
with the garlic, saffron, and salt and pepper. Add the
vegetables, grip the top edge of the bag to seal, and
toss together. Set aside for at least 30 minutes.

Make the rouille. Put the tomatoes and red bell pepper
into a small roasting pan. Sprinkle with the garlic,
pimenton, and salt and pepper, then drizzle the oil over.
Roast in a preheated oven, 425°F, for 15 minutes.

Cool, then peel the skins from the tomatoes and
pepper. Puree the flesh in a liquidizer or food processor
with any juices from the roasting pan until smooth.
Spoon into a serving bowl and set aside.

Put the saffron vegetables into a large roasting
pan and cook in a preheated oven, 425°F, for
15–20 minutes, turning once until browned. Spoon
the vegetables onto individual plates and serve with
spoonfuls of the rouille, reheated if necessary.

For potato puffs, to serve with the rouille instead of
the saffron vegetables, cut 2 lb new potatoes in half
and lay them, cutside uppermost, in a single layer in
an ovenproof dish. Scatter with sea salt and black
pepper and roast (without any oil) in a preheated
oven, 425°F, for 30–35 minutes, until cooked through
and puffed up. Serve with the rouille.

sweet potatoes & tomato salsa

Calories per serving **384**
Serves **2**
Preparation time **5 minutes**
Cooking time **45 minutes**

2 large **sweet potatoes**,
 about 9 oz each
½ cup grated **Swiss** or
 cheddar cheese,
salt

Tomato salsa
2 large **tomatoes**, finely
 chopped
½ small **red onion**, finely
 chopped
1 **celery stick**, finely chopped
small handful of **cilantro**,
 chopped
2 tablespoons **lime juice**
2 teaspoons **superfine sugar**

Scrub the potatoes and put them in a small roasting pan. Prick with a fork and sprinkle with a little salt. Bake in a preheated oven, 400°F, for 45 minutes, until tender. (If you do not have the time to bake the sweet potatoes, they can be microwaved like ordinary ones, although this way you will lose the wonderful crispy baked flavor. Prick them with a fork and cook on the highest setting for 15–20 minutes, or according to the manufacturer's instructions.)

Meanwhile, make the salsa. Mix the tomatoes in a bowl with the onion, celery, cilantro, lime juice, and sugar.

Halve the potatoes and fluff up the flesh with a fork. Sprinkle with the cheese and serve topped with the salsa.

For sweet potatoes with cilantro dressing, bake the potatoes as above. Omit the tomato salsa and cheese. Make a dressing by combining scant ½ cup crème fraîche or sour cream, 4 sliced scallions, a handful of chopped cilantro, and the rind and juice of 1 lime. Plate and fluff up the halved potatoes and serve with a generous dollop of dressing.

green bean & asparagus salad

Calories per serving **285**
Serves **6**
Preparation time **10 minutes**
Cooking time **8 minutes**

8 oz **fine green beans**,
   trimmed
13 oz fresh **asparagus**,
   trimmed
6 **eggs**
5 tablespoons **olive oil**
3 teaspoons **black olive
   pesto** or **tapenade**
3 teaspoons **balsamic
   vinegar**
5 cups **arugula**, rinsed
½ cup **pitted black olives**
3 oz **Parmesan cheese**, cut
   into shavings
salt and **black pepper**

Put the green beans in the top of a steamer, cover, and cook for 3 minutes. Add the asparagus and cook for 5 minutes, until the vegetables are just tender.

Meanwhile, put the eggs into a small saucepan, cover with cold water, and bring to a boil. Simmer for 6 minutes, until still soft in the center.

Mix together the oil, pesto, and vinegar in a small bowl with a little salt and pepper.

Arrange the arugula in the center of six serving plates. Drain and rinse the eggs with cold water. Drain again, gently peel away the shells, and halve each egg. Place two halves on each mound of arugula. Arrange the beans and asparagus around the edge, then drizzle with the dressing. Add the olives and top with the Parmesan shavings. Serve immediately.

For tenderstem broccoli & olive salad, omit the beans and asparagus and steam 1 lb tenderstem broccoli for 5 minutes. Cook the eggs as above, shell and quarter. Arrange the arugula on 6 plates, then scatter with the eggs and broccoli. Complete the recipe with the dressing, olives, and Parmesan, as above.

potato & onion tortilla

Calories per serving **296**
Serves **6**
Preparation time **10 minutes**
Cooking time **30 minutes**

1½ lb **baking potatoes**
4 tablespoons **olive oil**
2 large **onions**, thinly sliced
6 **eggs**, beaten
salt and **black pepper**

Slice the potatoes very thinly and toss them in a bowl with a little seasoning. Heat the oil in a medium-size, heavy skillet. Add the potatoes and fry them very gently for 10 minutes, turning them frequently until they are softened but not browned.

Add the onions and fry them gently for an additional 5 minutes without browning. Spread the potatoes and onions in an even layer in the skillet and turn the heat down as low as possible.

Pour over the eggs, cover, and cook very gently for about 15 minutes, until the eggs have set. (If the center of the omelet is too wet, put the skillet under a moderate broiler to finish cooking.) Turn the tortilla onto a plate and serve warm or cold.

For potato & artichoke tortilla, drain 3½ oz marinated artichokes in olive oil, reserving the oil. Cook the potatoes as above, replacing the olive oil with ¼ cup of the reserved oil. Roughly chop the artichokes and add to the pan with the onions and 1 tablespoon chopped mint. Complete the recipe as above.

tomato, tofu & hot pepper salad

Calories per serving **418**
Serves **2**
Preparation time **10 minutes**

1 large **beefsteak tomato**,
  thinly sliced
4 oz **tofu**
2 oz **hot piquante bell
  peppers**, drained and thinly
  sliced
3 tablespoons snipped **chives**
2 tablespoons chopped **flat-
  leaf parsley**
3 tablespoons **pine nuts**,
  toasted
¼ cup **golden raisins**
¼ cup **olive oil**
2 tablespoons **lemon juice**
2 teaspoons **superfine sugar**
salt and **pepper**

Arrange the tomato slices on two serving plates, lightly seasoning the layers with salt and pepper. Crumble the tofu into a mixing bowl, then add the hot piquante peppers, chives, parsley, pine nuts, and golden raisins and mix together.

Whisk together the olive oil, lemon juice, and sugar in a small pitcher or bowl. Season lightly with salt and pepper and mix into the salad.

Spoon the salad over the sliced tomatoes.

For spinach & tofu salad, omit the tomato and piquante bell peppers. Crumble the tofu as above, and add the herbs, pine nuts, golden raisins, and juice of 1 lime. Omit the olive oil, lemon juice, and superfine sugar. Heat 2 teaspoons peanut oil in a large skillet. Add 1 crushed garlic clove, cook for a few seconds, then add 8 oz baby spinach. Cook until wilted, then toss into the tofu salad and serve.

gingered tofu & mango salad

Calories per serving **340**
Serves **2**
Preparation time **15 minutes**,
  plus marinating
Cooking time **5 minutes**

4 oz **tofu**
¾ inch piece **fresh ginger
  root**, grated
2 tablespoons **light soy
  sauce**
1 **garlic clove**, crushed
1 tablespoon **seasoned rice
  vinegar**
2 tablespoons **peanut** or
  vegetable oil
1 bunch **scallions**, sliced
  diagonally into ¾ inch
  lengths
⅓ cup **cashew nuts**
1 small **mango**, halved, pitted,
  and sliced
½ small **iceberg lettuce**,
  shredded
2 tablespoons **water**

Pat the tofu dry on paper towels and cut into ½ inch
cubes. In a small bowl, mix together the ginger, soy
sauce, garlic, and vinegar. Add the tofu to the bowl and
toss the ingredients together. Set aside
to marinate for 15 minutes.

Lift the tofu from the marinade with a fork, drain it, and
reserve the marinade. Heat the oil in a skillet and
gently fry the tofu pieces for about 3 minutes, until
golden. Drain and keep them warm.

Add the scallions and cashew nuts to the pan and fry
quickly for 30 seconds. Add the mango slices to the
pan and cook for 30 seconds, until heated through.

Pile the lettuce onto serving plates and scatter the
tofu, scallions, mango, and cashew nuts over the top.
Heat the marinade juices in the pan with the water,
pour the mixture over the salad, and serve immediately.

For tofu & sugar snap salad, marinate and fry the
tofu as above. Add the scallions and cashew nuts to
the pan, also adding 1 red chile, sliced into rounds,
and 1½ cups halved sugar snap peas. Omit the
mango. Fry for 1 minute, until heated through, then
gently toss in the fried tofu. Add the juice of ½ lime
and the water to the reserved marinade and drizzle it
over the salad before serving on the lettuce.

red pepper & scallion dip

Calories per serving (dip only)
60
Serves **4**
Preparation time **10 minutes**
Cooking time **30–40 minutes**

1 large **red pepper**, cut into
  quarters, cored, and seeded
2 **garlic cloves**, unpeeled
1 cup **plain yogurt**
2 **scallions**, finely chopped
freshly ground **black pepper**
selection of **raw vegetables**,
  such as carrots, cucumber,
  bell peppers, fennel,
  tomatoes, baby corn, snow
  peas, celery, and zucchini,
  cut into batons, to serve

Slightly flatten the pepper quarters and place on a baking sheet. Wrap the garlic in foil and place on the sheet. Roast in a preheated oven, 425°F, for 30–40 minutes, until the pepper is slightly charred and the garlic is soft.

When cool enough to handle, remove the skin from the pepper and discard. Transfer the flesh to a bowl.

Squeeze the roasted garlic flesh from the cloves into the bowl.

Using a fork, roughly mash the bell pepper and garlic together. Stir in the yogurt and scallions. Season with pepper and serve with the vegetable batons.

For eggplant & yogurt dip, roast a whole eggplant in a preheated oven, 425°F, with the garlic for 30–40 minutes, omitting the red bell pepper. If the eggplant is still not tender after the cooking time, carefully turn it over and bake for an additional 10–15 minutes, until very soft. Cut the eggplant in half and scoop the flesh out onto a cutting board. Roughly chop with a handful of basil leaves and season with salt and pepper. Stir into the yogurt and scallions, and add the roasted garlic. Serve with the vegetable batons.

main meals
under 400 calories

cheesy pork with parsnip puree

Calories per serving **382**
Serves **4**
Preparation time **10 minutes**
Cooking time **25–30 minutes**

4 lean **pork steaks**, about
  4 oz each
1 teaspoon **olive oil**
2 oz **crumbly cheese**, such as
  Cheshire, crumbled
½ tablespoon chopped **sage**
1½ cups fresh **whole-grain
  bread crumbs**
1 **egg yolk**, beaten
black pepper

Parsnip puree
4¾ cups chopped **parsnips**,
  about 1¼ lb
2 **garlic cloves**
3 tablespoons **crème fraîche**
  or **sour cream**

Season the pork steaks with plenty of black pepper. Heat the oil in a nonstick skillet, add the pork steaks, and fry for 2 minutes on each side, until browned, then transfer to an ovenproof dish.

Mix together the cheese, sage, bread crumbs, and egg yolk. Divide the mixture into four and use to top each of the pork steaks, pressing down gently. Cook in a preheated oven, 400°F, for 12–15 minutes, until the topping is golden.

Meanwhile, make the puree. Place the parsnips and garlic in a saucepan of boiling water and cook for 10–12 minutes, until tender.

Drain and mash with the crème fraîche and plenty of black pepper. Serve with the pork steaks and some steamed green beans or cabbage.

For chicken with breaded tomato topping, replace the pork with 4 chicken fillets. Brown and lay in an ovenproof dish, as above. Make the topping as above, replacing the sage with 4 chopped sundried tomatoes and ¼ teaspoon dried oregano. Bake as above and serve with the parsnip puree.

chicken with soy glaze

Calories per serving **308**
Serves **4**
Preparation time **10 minutes**,
    plus chilling
Cooking time **30 minutes**

4 **chicken breasts**
4 tablespoons **dark soy
    sauce**
3 tablespoons **light brown
    sugar**
2 **garlic cloves**, crushed
2 tablespoons **white wine
    vinegar**
scant ½ cup **freshly
    squeezed orange juice**
black pepper

Lay the chicken breasts on a cutting board and slice each in half horizontally. Place in a large, shallow ovenproof dish, in which the chicken will fit snugly.

Mix together the soy sauce, sugar, garlic, vinegar, orange juice, and black pepper and pour the mixture over the chicken. Cover and chill the dish until you are ready to cook it.

Uncover the dish and bake the chicken in a preheated oven, 350°F, for 30 minutes, until it is cooked through. Transfer to serving plates and spoon the cooking juices over the meat.

Serve with steamed vegetables and rice or noodles.

For pork with oriental-style glaze, omit the chicken and lay 4 lean pork tenderloins in a shallow ovenproof dish. Combine the ingredients for the dressing as above, omitting the orange juice and adding 2 teaspoons chopped ginger and 2 tablespoons Chinese cooking wine or dry sherry. Cook in a preheated oven, 400°F, for 15 minutes, then serve with a scattering of cilantro leaves, steamed vegetables, and rice or noodles.

chorizo & red pepper stew

Calories per serving **369**
Serves **4**
Preparation time **5 minutes**
Cooking time **25 minutes**

1 lb **new potatoes**
1 teaspoon **olive oil**
2 **red onions**, chopped
2 **red bell peppers**, cored,
seeded and chopped
3½ oz **chorizo sausage**, thinly
sliced
1 lb **plum tomatoes**,
chopped, or a 13 oz can
tomatoes, drained
13 oz can **chickpeas**, drained
and rinsed
2 tablespoons chopped
parsley

Place the potatoes in a saucepan of boiling water and cook for 12–15 minutes, until tender. Drain, then slice.

Meanwhile, heat the oil in a large skillet, add the onions and bell peppers and fry for 3–4 minutes, until beginning to soften. Add the chorizo and continue to fry for 2 minutes.

Add the potato slices, tomatoes, and chickpeas, bring to a boil, and simmer for 10 minutes. Scatter over the parsley and serve with some crusty bread to mop up all the juices.

For Mediterranean vegetable stew, slice the raw potatoes and cut 1 eggplant and 1 zucchini into chunks. Fry the onions and bell peppers in the oil, as above, for 5 minutes. Omit the chorizo, and add in the prepared raw vegetables, tomatoes, and chickpeas. Add ⅔ cup Vegetable Stock (see page 44) and 2 sprigs thyme, and bring to a boil. Simmer for 15 minutes and scatter with the parsley. Drizzle with extravirgin olive oil, if liked, and serve with crusty bread.

wild rice jambalaya

Calories per serving **370**
Serves **4**
Preparation time **15 minutes**
Cooking time **35 minutes**

¾ cup **wild rice**
1 teaspoon **olive oil**
½ cup chopped **celery**
½ **red bell pepper**, cored, seeded, and diced
½ **green** or **yellow bell pepper**, cored, seeded, and diced
1 **onion**, chopped
1 **rindless lean Canadian bacon slice**, trimmed of fat
2 **garlic cloves**, crushed
2 tablespoons **tomato paste**
1 tablespoon chopped **thyme**
⅔ cup **long-grain rice**
1 **green chile**, seeded and finely chopped
½ teaspoon **cayenne pepper**
13 oz can **tomatoes**, drained
1¼ cups **chicken stock**
⅔ cup **dry white wine**
8 oz medium **shrimp**
cilantro or **parsley**, to garnish

Place the wild rice in a saucepan with water to cover. Bring to a boil and boil for 5 minutes. Remove the pan from the heat and cover tightly. Let stand to steam for about 10 minutes, until the grains are tender. Drain.

Heat the oil in a large nonstick skillet. Add the celery, bell peppers, onion, bacon, and garlic. Cook, stirring, for 3–4 minutes, until the vegetables are soft. Stir in the tomato paste and thyme. Cook for another 2 minutes.

Add the wild rice, long-grain rice, chile, cayenne pepper, tomatoes, stock, and wine. Bring to a boil. Reduce the heat and simmer for 10 minutes, until the rice is tender but still firm to the bite.

Add the shrimp and cook, stirring occasionally, for 5 minutes, until the shrimp have turned opaque. Spoon into large warmed bowls. Scatter with cilantro or parsley and serve with crusty bread, if liked.

For chicken & prawn jambalaya, omit the wild rice and increase the quantity of long-grain rice to 1⅓ cups. Soften the celery, bell peppers, onion, and garlic as above, omitting the bacon. Remove from the skillet and heat 1 tablespoon of olive oil in the same skillet. Add 4 oz chicken breast, cut into chunks, and fry until golden on all sides. Return the softened vegetables to the skillet, then add the remaining ingredients up to and including the white wine. Bring to a boil, then complete the recipe as above.

lean lasagna

Calories per serving **340**
Serves **8**
Preparation time **30 minutes**
Cooking time **about 1 hour**

7 oz **lasagna sheets**
freshly ground **black pepper**

Meat sauce
2 **eggplants**, peeled and
  diced
2 **red onions**, chopped
2 **garlic cloves**, crushed
1¼ cups **Vegetable Stock**
  (see page 44)
¼ cup **red wine**
1 lb **extra-lean ground beef**
two 13 oz cans **chopped
  tomatoes**

Cheese sauce
3 **egg whites**
8 oz **ricotta cheese**
¾ cup **milk**
generous ⅓ cup freshly grated
  Parmesan cheese

Cook the lasagna sheets as on package instructions.

Make the meat sauce. Place the eggplants, onions, garlic, stock, and wine in a large nonstick saucepan. Cover and simmer briskly for 5 minutes.

Uncover and cook for about 5 minutes, until the eggplant is tender and the liquid is absorbed, adding a little more stock if necessary. Remove from the heat, let cool slightly, then puree in a food processor or blender.

Meanwhile, brown the beef in a nonstick skillet. Skim off any fat. Add the eggplant mixture, tomatoes, and black pepper to taste. Simmer briskly, uncovered, for about 10 minutes, until thickened.

Make the cheese sauce. Beat the egg whites with the ricotta, then beat in the milk and ¼ cup of Parmesan. Season with black pepper to taste.

Alternate layers of meat sauce, cooked lasagna, and cheese sauce in an ovenproof dish. Start with meat sauce and finish with cheese sauce. Sprinkle the top layer of cheese sauce with the remaining Parmesan. Bake in a preheated oven, 350°F, for 30–40 minutes, until browned.

For lean vegetarian lasagna, cook the eggplants, onions, garlic, stock, and wine as above, also adding 1 chopped carrot, 1 thinly sliced celery stick, and 1¾ cups diced butternut squash or pumpkin. Cook as above but do not puree. Add the tomatoes and simmer for 10 minutes. Omit the beef. Make the cheese sauce and complete the recipe as above.

haddock with poached eggs

Calories per serving **397**
Serves **4**
Preparation time **10 minutes**
Cooking time **30 minutes**

1½ lb **new potatoes**
4 **scallions**, sliced
2 tablespoons **crème fraîche**
   or **sour cream**
3 oz **watercress**
4 **smoked haddock fillets**,
   about 5 oz each
⅔ cup **milk**
1 **bay leaf**
4 **eggs**
black pepper

Place the potatoes in a saucepan of boiling water and cook for 12–15 minutes, until tender. Drain, lightly crush with a fork, then stir through the scallions, crème fraîche, and watercress and season well with black pepper. Keep warm.

Put the fish and milk in a large skillet with the bay leaf. Bring to a boil, then cover and simmer for 5–6 minutes, until the fish is cooked through.

Meanwhile, bring a saucepan of water to a boil, swirl the water with a spoon, and crack in an egg, letting the white to wrap around the yolk. Simmer for 3 minutes, then remove and keep warm. Repeat with the remaining eggs.

Serve the haddock on top of the potatoes, topped with the poached eggs.

For haddock, asparagus & egg salad, replace the new potatoes with 11 oz asparagus and cook in boiling water for 5 minutes. Stir into a bowl with the scallions, crème fraîche, and watercress, adding the leaves of a baby gem lettuce and 1 tablespoon extravirgin olive oil. Poach the haddock as above, remove from the milk with a slotted spoon, and break into flakes. Toss the fish in the asparagus salad and divide between 4 plates. Serve with a poached egg on top, prepared as above.

honey-glazed tuna

Calories per serving **310**
Serves **4**
Preparation time **15 minutes**
Cooking time **15 minutes**

4 **tuna steaks**, about 4 oz
  each
2 teaspoons **olive oil**

Glaze
1 tablespoon **honey**
2 tablespoons **whole-grain
  mustard**
1 teaspoon **tomato paste**
2 tablespoons **orange juice**
1 tablespoon **red wine
  vinegar** or **balsamic
  vinegar**
freshly ground **black pepper**

Parsnip puree
2 **parsnips**, cut into chunks
2 **potatoes**, cut into chunks
¼ cup **plain yogurt**
2 teaspoons **horseradish
  relish** (optional)
freshly ground **black pepper**

Place all the ingredients for the glaze in a small saucepan. Bring to a boil, then reduce the heat and simmer until the mixture reduces and is of a glaze consistency. Keep hot.

Make the parsnip puree. Steam the parsnips and potatoes until tender. Drain, if necessary, and place in a food processor or blender with the yogurt, horseradish relish (if using), and black pepper to taste. Process until blended. Keep warm or reheat prior to serving.

Brush the tuna with the oil. Cook on a preheated, very hot grill pan or barbecue, or in a skillet or under a broiler, for 1–2 minutes. Turn and spoon the glaze over the tuna. Cook for another 1–2 minutes—it is best if moist and still slightly pink in the center.

To serve, top a mound of the parsnip puree with a tuna steak and spoon over the remaining glaze. Serve with steamed green vegetables, if liked.

For peppered tuna with watercress & parsnip puree, omit the glaze ingredients and coat the tuna steaks with 2 tablespoons roughly crushed peppercorns. Blend 3 oz watercress in a food processor with 1 crushed garlic clove, 2 tablespoons skim milk, and salt to make a paste. Cook the puree as above, then fold in the watercress paste. Brush the tuna in oil and cook as above. Serve with the puree and steamed vegetables, if liked.

salmon with bean & celeriac mash

Calories per serving **399**
Serves **4**
Preparation time **15 minutes**
Cooking time **20 minutes**

scant ¾ cup **cooked soybeans**
3 tablespoons **water**
½ medium **celeriac**, about 8 oz
1 medium **potato**, cut into chunks
4 **salmon fillets**, about 4 oz each
3 tablespoons **butter**
3 tablespoons chopped **chives**
3 tablespoons chopped **tarragon** or **dill**
1 tablespoon **white wine vinegar**
salt and **black pepper**

Put the cooked beans and measured water in a food processor and blend them to a smooth paste. Cut away the skin from the celeriac, cut the flesh into chunks, and cook them in a saucepan of lightly salted boiling water, with the potatoes, for about 15 minutes, until tender.

Meanwhile, pat the salmon fillets dry on paper towels and season them with salt and pepper. Heat 1 tablespoon of the butter in a skillet and fry the salmon for 4–5 minutes on each side, until it is cooked through.

Drain the vegetables and return them to the saucepan with the blended beans and another 1 tablespoon of the butter. Using a potato masher, mash the ingredients together until evenly combined. Reheat for 1–2 minutes and season with salt and pepper.

Pile the mash onto warmed serving plates and top with the salmon fillets. Add the remaining butter, herbs, and vinegar to the skillet and heat through until the mixture bubbles. Pour the sauce over the salmon and serve immediately.

For a soybean, pea, & dill salad, to serve with the salmon instead of the mash, cook scant ⅔ cup frozen soy beans and generous 1 cup frozen peas in salted boiling water for 3–4 minutes, until just tender. Drain and stir into a dressing made of 1 tablespoon olive oil, 1 teaspoon honey, 1 teaspoon white wine vinegar, and 1 tablespoon chopped dill. Cook the salmon as above, reducing the quantity of herbs in the sauce to 1 tablespoon.

sesame-crusted salmon

Calories per serving **324**
Serves **4**
Preparation time **10 minutes**
Cooking time **12 minutes**

4 tablespoons **sesame seeds**
1 teaspoon **dried chili flakes**
4 **salmon fillets**, about 3½ oz
  each
2 teaspoons **olive oil**
2 **carrots**, cut into matchsticks
2 **red bell peppers**, cored,
  seeded and thinly sliced
7 oz **shiitake mushrooms**,
  halved
2 **bok choy**, quartered
  lengthwise
4 **scallions**, shredded
1 tablespoon **soy sauce**

Mix together the sesame seeds and chili flakes on a plate, then press the salmon fillets into this mixture to cover.

Heat half the oil in a nonstick skillet or wok, add the salmon, and cook over a medium heat for 3–4 minutes on each side, until cooked through. Set the salmon aside, keeping it warm.

Heat the remaining oil in the skillet, then add the vegetables and quickly stir-fry for 3–4 minutes, until just cooked. Drizzle the soy sauce over the vegetables, then serve with the salmon and basmati rice.

For an oriental-style vegetable & salmon soup, make a soup base by heating 3 cups Vegetable Stock (see page 44) in a pan with 3 slices ginger, 2 tablespoons dark soy sauce, 2 tablespoons Chinese cooking wine or dry sherry, and 1 teaspoon sesame oil. Bring to a boil and simmer while you cook the salmon and vegetables as above. Break the salmon into flakes and stir into the soup with the stir-fried vegetables.

lentils with flaked salmon

Calories per serving **382**
Serves **4**
Preparation time **30 minutes**,
 plus cooling and chilling
Cooking time **45 minutes**

1 lb **salmon tail fillet**
2 tablespoons **dry white wine**
2 **red bell peppers**, halved,
 cored and seeded
⅔ cup **French green lentils**,
 well rinsed
large handful of **dill**, chopped
1 bunch of **scallions**, finely
 sliced
lemon juice, for squeezing
freshly ground **black pepper**

Dressing
2 **garlic cloves**
large handful of **flat-leaf**
 parsley, chopped
large handful of **dill**, chopped
1 teaspoon **Dijon mustard**
2 **green chiles**, seeded and
 chopped
juice of 2 large **lemons**
1 tablespoon **extravirgin olive**
 oil

Place the salmon on a sheet of foil and spoon over the wine. Gather up the foil and fold over at the top to seal. Place on a baking sheet and bake in a preheated oven, 400°F, for 15–20 minutes, until cooked. Let cool, then flake, cover, and chill.

Broil the bell peppers, skin-side up, under a preheated hot broiler until charred. Put in a plastic bag for a few minutes. Remove from the bag, peel off the skin, and cut the flesh into 1 inch cubes, reserving any juices.

Place all the dressing ingredients, except the oil, in a food processor or blender and process until smooth. While blending, drizzle in the oil until the mixture is thick.

Put the lentils in a large saucepan with plenty of water, bring to a boil, then simmer gently for about 15–20 minutes, until cooked but still firm to the bite. Drain and place in a bowl with the red bell pepper, dill, most of the scallions, and black pepper to taste.

Stir the dressing into the hot lentils. To serve, top the lentils with the flaked salmon and gently mix through the lentils and dressing, squeeze over a little lemon juice and scatter with the remaining scallions.

For smoked mackerel & lentil salad, omit the salmon and wine, cook the bell peppers and lentils as above, and combine in a bowl with the dill and all the scallions. Heat 2 teaspoons olive oil in a nonstick skillet and fry 2 bacon slices, cut into strips, until crispy. Add to the bowl. Combine the ingredients for the dressing and toss into the bowl, (crush the garlic). Gently fold 13 oz flaked smoked mackerel through the salad and serve.

baked eggplant with tzatziki

Calories per serving **325**
Serves **4**
Preparation time **10 minutes**,
  plus cooling
Cooking time **50 minutes**

2 large **eggplants**, halved
  lengthwise
1 tablespoon **olive oil**
generous ½ cup **couscous**
¾ cup **boiling water**
1 **onion**, finely chopped
1 **garlic clove**, crushed
generous ½ cup **dried
  apricots**, chopped
⅓ cup **raisins**
grated rind and juice of
  1 **lemon**
2 tablespoons chopped **mint**
2 tablespoons chopped
  cilantro
2 tablespoons freshly grated
  Parmesan cheese
4 **flat breads**, to serve

Tzatziki
½ **cucumber**, finely chopped
2 **scallions**, sliced
scant 1 cup **Greek yogurt**

Place the eggplants cut side up on a baking sheet and brush each with a little of the oil. Cook in a preheated oven, 400°F, for 30–35 minutes, until the flesh is tender, then remove (leaving the oven on) and let cool. When the eggplants are cool enough to touch, scoop out the flesh and roughly chop. Reserve the skins.

Meanwhile, place the couscous in a heatproof container, pour on the measured water, and cover with plastic wrap. Set aside for 5 minutes, then remove the plastic wrap and fork through.

Heat the remaining oil in a nonstick skillet, add the onion and garlic, and fry for 3 minutes, then stir through the apricots, raisins, lemon rind and juice, couscous, herbs, Parmesan, and eggplant flesh.

Spoon this mixture into the eggplant skins and return them to the oven for 10 minutes.

Mix together the tzatziki ingredients in a serving bowl and serve with the eggplants and flat breads.

For a spiced tomato sauce, to serve with the eggplants instead of the tzatziki, heat 2 teaspoons olive oil in a saucepan and use to cook 1 sliced onion for 5 minutes, until beginning to soften. Add ½ teaspoon each ground cinnamon, ground cumin, and ground ginger and cook for 1 additional minute. Stir in a 13 oz can chopped tomatoes and bring to a boil. Simmer uncovered for 20 minutes, then remove from the heat and season with salt and harissa paste to taste. Serve warm or at room temperature.

stir-fried tofu with shrimp

Calories per serving **390**
Serves **2**
Preparation time **10 minutes**,
  plus standing
Cooking time **10 minutes**

8 oz **tofu**
3 tablespoons **soy sauce**
1 tablespoon **honey**
1 tablespoon **soy** or **peanut oil**
1½ cups shredded **collard greens**
1¾ cups **cooked rice noodles**
7 oz **cooked, peeled shrimp**
4 tablespoons **hoisin sauce**
2 tablespoons chopped **cilantro**

Pat the tofu dry on paper towels and cut into ¾ inch dice. Mix the soy sauce and honey together in a small bowl, then add the tofu and mix gently. Let stand for 5 minutes.

Drain the tofu, reserving the marinade, and pat the cubes dry on paper towels. Heat the oil in a large skillet and fry the tofu for 5 minutes, stirring, until it is crisp and golden. Drain the pieces and keep them warm.

Add the greens to the skillet and fry them quickly, stirring, until they are wilted. Return the tofu to the skillet with the noodles and shrimp and cook them briskly, tossing the ingredients together, for 2 minutes.

Mix the hoisin sauce with the reserved marinade. Drizzle the liquid over the stir-fry, mix it in, scatter over the fresh cilantro and serve immediately.

For cold tofu & noodle salad, cut and marinate the tofu as above, also adding 4 sliced scallions and 1 seeded and chopped red chile, and increase the marinating time to at least 1 hour. Pour the marinade into a large bowl and toss in the peanut oil, rice noodles, shrimp, and cilantro. Add 1 cup shredded sugar snap peas and gently fold in the tofu. Serve, omitting the hoisin sauce.

main meals
under 300 calories

lamb cutlets with herbed crust

Calories per serving **280**
Serves **4**
Preparation time **10 minutes**
Cooking time **15 minutes**

12 lean **lamb cutlets**, about
  1½ oz each
2 tablespoons **pesto**
3 tablespoons **wholegrain
  bread crumbs**
1 tablespoon chopped
  walnuts, toasted
1 teaspoon **vegetable oil**
2 **garlic cloves**, crushed
1¼ lb **collard greens**, finely
  shredded and blanched

Heat a nonstick skillet or grill pan until hot, add the cutlets and cook for 1 minute on each side, then transfer to a baking sheet.

Mix together the pesto, bread crumbs, and walnuts and use to top one side of the cutlets, pressing down lightly. Cook in a preheated oven, 400°F, for 10–12 minutes.

Meanwhile, heat the oil in a skillet or wok, add the garlic, and stir-fry for 1 minute, then add the collard greens and continue to stir-fry for 3–4 minutes, until tender.

Serve the lamb and collard greens along with some baby carrots.

For lamb cutlets with a herbed caper dressing, make a dressing by combining 1 tablespoon each chopped flat-leaf parsley, mint, and basil. Stir in 1 crushed garlic clove, 1 tablespoon chopped capers, and 2 tablespoons extravirgin olive oil. Grill the cutlets for 2–3 minutes on each side, depending on whether you like your lamb medium or well done, omit the bread-crumb topping, and serve with the vegetables as above and a generous drizzle of the dressing.

lamb & bean stew

Calories per serving **288**
Serves **4**
Preparation time **5 minutes**
Cooking time **1 hour 20 minutes**

1 teaspoon **olive oil**
11½ oz lean **lamb**, cubed
16 **pearl onions**, peeled
1 **garlic clove**, crushed
1 tablespoon **all-purpose flour**
2½ cups **lamb stock** (made with concentrated liquid stock)
7 oz can **chopped tomatoes**
1 **bouquet garni**
two 13 oz cans **flageolet** or **cannellini eans**, drained and rinsed
1⅔ cups **cherry tomatoes**, about 8 oz
black pepper

Heat the oil in a flameproof casserole or saucepan, add the lamb, and fry for 3–4 minutes, until browned all over. Remove the lamb from the casserole and set aside.

Add the onions and garlic to the pan and fry for 4–5 minutes, until the onions are beginning to brown.

Return the lamb and any juices to the pan, then stir through the flour and add the stock, tomatoes, bouquet garni, and beans. Bring to a boil, stirring, then cover and simmer for 1 hour, until the lamb is just tender.

Add the cherry tomatoes to the dish and season well with pepper. Continue to simmer for 10 minutes, then serve with steamed potatoes and green beans.

For pork & cider warming pot, replace the lamb with 11½ oz pork tenderloin, cubed. Brown as above and set aside. Cook the onion and garlic as above, add the browned pork and stir in the flour. Pour in 1⅔ cups each ham stock and hard cider, instead of the lamb stock. Omit the canned tomatoes, and add the bouquet garni and beans. Simmer covered as above, adding 2⅓ cups cubed carrots to the pan 30 minutes into cooking. Simmer for another 30 minutes, omitting the cherry tomatoes. Remove from the heat and stir in 2 tablespoons whole-grain mustard and a handful of chopped flat-leaf parsley.

beef skewers with dipping sauce

Calories per serving **140**
Serves **4**
Preparation time **10 minutes**,
  plus marinating
Cooking time **5 minutes**

1 tablespoon **sweet chili
  sauce**
½ teaspoon **cumin seeds**,
  toasted
½ teaspoon **ground coriander**
1 teaspoon **olive oil**
11½ oz lean **round steak**, cut
  into strips

Dipping sauce
1 tablespoon **sweet chili
  sauce**
1 teaspoon **Thai fish sauce**
1 teaspoon **white wine
  vinegar**

To serve
2 tablespoons chopped
  cilantro
1 tablespoon **unsalted
  peanuts**, roughly chopped
  (optional)

Mix together the sweet chili sauce, cumin seeds, ground coriander and oil in a nonmetallic bowl. Add the meat and stir well to coat, then cover and let marinate in a cool place for 30 minutes.

Thread the meat onto four bamboo skewers that have been soaked in water for at least 20 minutes. Cook on a hot grill pan or under a high broiler for 2–3 minutes, until cooked through.

Meanwhile, mix together the sauce ingredients in a small serving bowl. Serve the skewers with the sauce, scattered with the cilantro and peanuts, if desired.

For a Thai-style salad, to serve with the skewers, combine 1 grated carrot, ¼ thinly sliced cucumber, ½ cup raw bean sprouts, and 10 quartered cherry tomatoes. Make the dipping sauce as above, adding 1 tablespoon peanut oil. Toss it into the salad ingredients with the cilantro and peanuts used as garnish above, and serve the skewers with the salad and lime wedges.

thai beef & mixed pepper stir-fry

Calories per serving **255**
Serves **4**
Preparation time **20 minutes**
Cooking time **10 minutes**

1 lb lean **beef tenderloin fillet**
1 tablespoon **sesame oil**
1 **garlic clove**, finely chopped
1 **lemon grass stalk**, finely
  shredded
1 inch piece of **fresh ginger
  root**, peeled and finely
  chopped
1 **red bell pepper**, cored,
  seeded, and thickly sliced
1 **green bell pepper**, cored,
  seeded, and thickly sliced
1 **onion**, thickly sliced
2 tablespoons **lime juice**
freshly ground **black pepper**

Cut the beef into long, thin strips, cutting across the grain.

Heat the oil in a wok or large skillet over a high heat. Add the garlic and stir-fry for 1 minute. Add the beef and stir-fry for 2–3 minutes, until lightly colored. Stir in the lemon grass and ginger and remove the pan from the heat. Remove the beef from the skillet and set aside.

Add the bell peppers and onion to the skillet and stir-fry for 2–3 minutes, until the onions are just turning golden brown and are slightly softened.

Return the beef to the skillet, stir in the lime juice and season with black pepper to taste. Serve with boiled noodles or rice, if liked.

For coconut rice, to serve with the stir-fry, place 1¼ cups fragrant Thai rice in a heavy pan, pour in ⅔ cup reduced-fat coconut milk, and add enough water to come 1 inch above the level of the rice. Bring to a boil, then reduce the heat to a slow simmer and cover. Cook for 10 minutes, remove from the heat, and keep covered for another 10 minutes to finish cooking in its own heat. Fluff up with a fork and serve.

chicken tikka sticks & fennel raita

Calories per serving **179**
Serves **6**
Preparation time **20 minutes**,
  plus marinating and chilling
Cooking time **8–10 minutes**

1 **onion**, finely chopped
½–1 large **red** or **green chile**,
  seeded and finely chopped
  (to taste)
¾ inch piece of **fresh ginger
  root**, finely chopped
2 **garlic cloves**, finely
  chopped
⅔ cup **plain yogurt**
3 teaspoons **mild curry paste**
¼ cup chopped **cilantro**
4 **chicken breasts**, about
  5 oz each, cubed
shredded **lettuce**, to serve

Fennel raita
1 small **fennel bulb**, about
  7 oz
scant 1 cup **plain yogurt**
3 tablespoons chopped
  cilantro
salt and **black pepper**

Mix the onion, chile, ginger, and garlic together in a shallow china dish. Add the yogurt, curry paste, and cilantro, and mix together.

Add the cubed chicken to the yogurt mixture, mix to coat, cover with plastic wrap, and chill for at least 2 hours.

Make the raita. Cut the core away from the fennel and finely chop the remainder, including any green tops. Mix the fennel with the yogurt and cilantro and season with salt and pepper. Spoon the raita into a serving dish, cover with plastic wrap, and chill until needed.

Thread the chicken onto 12 skewers and place them on a foil-lined broiler rack. Cook under a preheated broiler for 8–10 minutes, turning once, until browned and the chicken is cooked through. Transfer to serving plates lined with a little shredded lettuce and serve with spoonfuls of the raita.

For a red pepper & almond chutney, to serve with the skewers instead of the raita, blend 3 oz store-bought roasted bell peppers in a blender or food processor, with a handful of mint leaves, 1 chopped garlic clove, and ½ teaspoon chili powder. Blend until smooth, then add salt to taste and 1½ tablespoons slivered, toasted almonds. Pulse a couple of times to roughly crush the almonds and stir in 1 tablespoon chopped cilantro.

one-pot chicken

Calories per serving **275**
Serves **4**
Preparation time **10 minutes**
Cooking time **45 minutes**

1 lb **new potatoes**
4 **chicken breasts**, about
  4 oz each
6 tablespoons **mixed herbs**,
  such as parsley, chives,
  chervil, and mint
1 **garlic clove**, crushed
6 tablespoons **crème fraîche**
  or **sour cream**
8 **baby leeks**
2 **Belgian endive** heads,
  halved lengthwise
⅔ cup **chicken stock**
black pepper

Place the potatoes in a saucepan of boiling water and cook for 12–15 minutes, until tender. Drain, then cut into bite-size pieces.

Make a slit lengthwise down the side of each chicken breast to form a pocket, ensuring that you do not cut all the way through. Mix together the herbs, garlic, and crème fraîche, season well with black pepper, then spoon a little into each chicken pocket.

Put the leeks, chicory, and potatoes in an ovenproof dish. Pour over the stock, then lay the chicken breasts on top. Spoon over the remaining crème fraîche mixture, then bake in a preheated oven, 400°F, for 25–30 minutes.

For baked chicken with fennel & potatoes, cut the potatoes in half and place them in a large ovenproof dish with 1 large fennel bulb, cut into quarters. Omit the leeks and Belgian endive. Pour over the stock and bake in a preheated oven at 400°F, for 20 minutes. Remove from the oven and lay the chicken breasts over the vegetables. Combine 1 tablespoon chopped parsley with 1 tablespoon Dijon mustard and the crème fraîche, omitting the garlic, and spoon the mixture over the chicken. Bake for another 25–30 minutes.

thai-style angler fish kebabs

Calories per serving **192**
Serves **4**
Preparation time **15 minutes**,
   plus marinating
Cooking time **10 minutes**

1–1½ lb **angler fish tails**,
   skinned
1 **onion**, quartered and layers
   separated
8 **mushrooms**
1 **zucchini**, cut into 8 pieces
vegetable oil, for brushing
watercress or **flat-leaf
   parsley**, to garnish

Marinade
grated rind and juice of
   2 **limes**
1 **garlic clove**, finely chopped
2 tablespoons finely sliced
   fresh ginger root
2 fresh **chiles**, red or green or
   1 of each, seeded and finely
   chopped
2 **lemon grass stalks**, finely
   chopped
handful of chopped **cilantro**
1 glass **red wine**
2 tablespoons **sesame oil**
freshly ground **black pepper**

Combine the ingredients for the marinade in a large bowl. Cut the fish into large cubes and add to the marinade with the onion, mushrooms, and zucchini. Cover and refrigerate for 1 hour to marinate.

Brush the rack of a broiler pan lightly with oil to prevent the kebabs from sticking. Thread four skewers with the chunks of fish, mushrooms, zucchini, and onion alternately. Brush with a little oil and broil under a preheated hot broiler for about 10 minutes, turning at intervals. Garnish with watercress or flat leaf-parsley.

For Mediterranean angler fish kebabs, replace the above marinade with one using the grated rind and juice of 1 lemon, 2 chopped garlic cloves, 3 tablespoons olive oil, and 1 tablespoon each chopped thyme and rosemary. Use to marinate the angler fish and vegetables for 30 minutes, then thread and cook as above.

flounder & mustard sauce

Calories per serving **182**
Serves **4**
Preparation time **10 minutes**
Cooking time **10 minutes**

1 teaspoon **olive oil**
1 small **onion**, finely chopped
1 **garlic clove**, crushed
4 **flounder** or **sole fillets**,
   about 5 oz each
½ cup **dry white wine**
2 tablespoons **whole-grain
   mustard**
1 scant cup **crème fraîche** or
   sour cream
2 tablespoons chopped
   mixed herbs

Heat the oil in a large skillet, add the onion and garlic, and fry for 3 minutes, until softened.

Add the fish fillets and cook for 1 minute on each side. Then add the wine and simmer to reduce by half.

Stir through the remaining ingredients, bring to a boil, and simmer for 3–4 minutes, until the sauce has thickened slightly and the fish is tender. Serve with rice or new potatoes and steamed vegetables.

For salmon with cucumber & crème fraîche, cook the onion and garlic as above. Omit the flounder or sole. Add 13 oz skinned salmon, cut into chunks, and cook, stirring, for 1 minute. Add the wine, simmer as above, then add 1 tablespoon whole-grain mustard, the crème fraîche and ¼ cucumber, peeled and sliced. Cook for 2 minutes, then stir in 1 tablespoon chopped dill instead of the mixed herbs.

scallops with white bean puree

Calories per serving **293**
Serves **4**
Preparation time **10 minutes**
Cooking time **15 minutes**

two 13 oz cans **cannellini
beans**, drained and rinsed
2 **garlic cloves**
scant 1 cup **Vegetable Stock**
(see page 44)
2 tablespoons chopped
parsley
2 teaspoons **olive oil**
16 **baby leeks**
3 tablespoons **water**
16 large **scallops**, shelled and
prepared

Place the beans, garlic, and stock in a saucepan, bring
to a boil, and simmer for 10 minutes. Remove from the
heat, drain off any excess liquid, then mash with a
potato masher and stir in the parsley. Keep warm.

Heat half the oil in a nonstick skillet, add the leeks,
and fry for 2 minutes, then add the measured water.
Cover and simmer for 5–6 minutes, until tender.

Meanwhile, heat the remaining oil in a small skillet,
add the scallops, and fry for 1 minute on each side.
Serve with the white bean puree and leeks.

**For prosciutto wrapped scallops with cheesy bean
puree**, make the puree as above, replacing the
parsley with 2 tablespoons freshly grated Parmesan
cheese. Remove the fat from 8 slices prosciutto and
cut them in half widthwise. Wrap one strip of
prosciutto around each scallop and season with salt
and black pepper. Omit the leeks. Heat all the oil in a
large nonstick skillet, cook the scallops for 2 minutes
on each side, and serve with the puree.

thai mussel curry with ginger

Calories per serving **230**
Serves **4**
Preparation time **30 minutes**
Cooking time **13 minutes**

½–1 large **red chile** (to taste)
2 **shallots**, quartered
1 **lemon grass stem**
1 inch piece of **fresh ginger root**, peeled and chopped
1 tablespoon **sunflower oil**
14 fl oz can **reduced-fat coconut milk**
4–5 **kaffir lime leaves**
⅔ cup **fish stock**
2 teaspoons **Thai fish sauce**
3 lb **fresh mussels**, soaked in cold water
small bunch of **cilantro**, torn into pieces, to garnish

Halve the chile and keep the seeds for extra heat, if liked. Put the chile, shallots, and lemon grass into a liquidizer with the ginger and process together until finely chopped.

Heat the oil in large, deep saucepan, add the finely chopped ingredients, and fry over a medium heat for 5 minutes, stirring until softened. Add the coconut milk, kaffir lime leaves, fish stock, and fish sauce and cook for 3 minutes. Set aside until ready to finish.

Meanwhile, pick over the mussels and discard any that are opened or have cracked shells. Scrub with a small nailbrush, remove any barnacles, and pull off the small, hairy beards. Put them in a bowl of clean water and leave until ready to cook.

Reheat the coconut milk mixture. Drain the mussels and add to the mixture. Cover the pan with a lid and cook for about 5 minutes, until the mussel shells have opened.

Spoon the mussels and the coconut sauce into bowls, discarding any mussels that have not opened. Garnish with the cilantro.

For Thai chicken & eggplant curry, prepare the above recipe up to the end of the second step. Omit the mussels. Pour in 1 cup chicken stock and bring to a boil. Stir in 1 diced eggplant and 10 oz chicken breast, cut into large chunks. Bring to a boil again, cover, and simmer for 12–15 minutes, until the chicken is cooked and the eggplant tender. Serve with a scattering of cilantro.

scallops with cilantro yogurt

Calories per serving **217**
Serves **2**
Preparation time **15 minutes**
Cooking time **5 minutes**

⅔ cup **plain yogurt**

2 tablespoons chopped **cilantro**

finely grated rind and juice of **1 lime**

2 teaspoons **sesame oil**

½ small **red onion**, finely chopped

½ inch piece **fresh ginger root**, grated

1 **garlic clove**, crushed

2 teaspoons **superfine sugar**

2 teaspoons **dark soy sauce**

1 tablespoon **water**

1 pointed **green bell pepper**, thinly sliced

12 large **scallops**

arugula, to serve

Mix together the yogurt, cilantro, and lime rind in a small bowl, then transfer to a serving dish.

Heat half of the oil in a small pan and gently fry the onion for 3 minutes, until it has softened. Remove the pan from the heat and add the ginger, garlic, sugar, soy sauce, measured water, and lime juice.

Brush a grill pan with the remaining oil. Add the green bell pepper and scallops, cook the scallops for 1 minute on each side, until cooked through, and the pepper for a little longer, if necessary.

Pile the bell pepper and scallops on to serving plates with the arugula. Heat the soy glaze through and spoon it over the scallops. Serve with the yogurt sauce.

For squid & arugula salad with sweet soy glaze, omit the scallops and green bell pepper. Make the yogurt and cilantro sauce and set aside. Heat 2 teaspoons peanut oil in a large wok or skillet over a high heat. Add 11½ oz raw squid rings and stir-fry for 1 minute before adding the onion, ginger, and garlic. Cook, stirring, for another 1 minute, then add the sugar, soy sauce, water, and only 1 teaspoon sesame oil. Stir for 30 seconds, then remove from the heat and serve on a bed of arugula with the yogurt and cilantro sauce on the side.

shrimp with tamarind & lime

Calories per serving **122**
Serves **6**
Preparation time **5 minutes**
Cooking time **10 minutes**

2 lb large, uncooked **jumbo
  shrimp** in their shells
  (thawed if frozen)
2 tablespoons **olive oil**
1 large **onion**, chopped
3–4 **garlic cloves**, finely
  chopped
1½ inch piece of **fresh ginger
  root**, peeled and finely
  chopped
2 teaspoons **tamarind paste**
juice of 2 **limes**
1¼ cups **fish stock**

To garnish
small bunch of **cilantro**, torn
  into pieces
lime wedges

Rinse the shrimp in cold water and drain well. Heat the
oil in a large saucepan or wok, add the onion, and fry
for 5 minutes, until just beginning to brown.

Stir in the garlic, ginger, and tamarind paste, then mix
in the lime juice and stock.

Bring the stock to a boil, add the shrimp, and cook,
stirring, for 5 minutes, until the shrimp are bright pink.
Spoon into bowls and serve garnished with the torn
cilantro leaves and lime wedges.

For shrimp with tomato & coconut, brown the
onions as above. Add the shrimp, garlic, and ginger
and fry until the shrimp turn pink, then add the lime
juice, 2 tablespoons tamarind paste, scant ½ cup
coconut milk, and 3 medium tomatoes, seeded and
finely chopped. Omit the stock. Bring to a boil and
simmer for 2 minutes, then serve with the cilantro and
lime garnish.

lobster with shallots & vermouth

Calories per serving **275**
Serves **4**
Preparation time **1 hour**
Cooking time **10–11 minutes**

2 **cooked lobsters**,
   1¼–1½ lb each
2 tablespoons **olive oil**
2 **shallots**, finely chopped
4 canned **anchovy fillets**,
   drained and finely chopped
6 tablespoons **dry vermouth**
6 tablespoons **crème fraîche**
   or **sour cream**
2–4 teaspoons **fresh lemon
   juice** (to taste)
black pepper

To garnish
paprika
arugula

Lay one of the lobsters on its back. Cut it in half, beginning at the head, down through the natural line between the claws, unfurling the tail as you cut downward until the lobster can be separated into two. Repeat with the second lobster. Take out the black, threadlike intestine that runs down the tail and the small whitish sac found in the top part of the head. Leave the greenish liver, as this is a great delicacy.

Twist off the big claws. Crack these open with poultry shears, a nutcracker, pestle, or rolling pin. Carefully peel away the shell and lift out the firm, white meat, discarding the hard, white, oval membrane that lies in the center of the claw. Twist off the small claws, being careful not to tear off any lobster meat from the body, and discard.

Scoop out the thick, white tail meat, slice, and reserve it. Slowly and carefully remove all the remaining lobster meat from the body, picking it over for stray pieces of shell and bone. Rinse the shells and put them on four serving plates.

Heat the oil in a large skillet, add the shallots and fry gently for 5 minutes, until softened and just beginning to color. Mix in the anchovies, vermouth, and black pepper and cook for 2 minutes.

Add the lobster meat and crème fraîche and heat through gently for 3–4 minutes. Stir in lemon juice to taste. Spoon into the lobster shells, sprinkle with paprika, and garnish with arugula.

pumpkin & goat cheese bake

Calories per serving **230**
Serves **4**
Preparation time **20 minutes**
Cooking time **25–30 minutes**

3 cups peeled and diced **beet**
1¼ lb **pumpkin** or **butternut squash**, peeled, seeded and cut into slightly larger dice
1 **red onion**, cut into wedges
2 tablespoons **olive oil**
2 teaspoons **fennel seeds**
2 small **goat cheeses**, 3½ oz each
salt and **black pepper**
chopped **rosemary**, to garnish

Put the beet, pumpkin, and onion into a roasting pan, drizzle with the oil, and sprinkle with the fennel seeds and salt and pepper. Roast the vegetables in a preheated oven, 400°F, for 20–25 minutes, turning once, until well browned and tender.

Cut the goat cheeses in half and nestle each half among the roasted vegetables. Sprinkle the cheeses with a little salt and pepper and drizzle with some of the pan juices.

Return the dish to the oven for about 5 minutes, until the cheese is just beginning to melt. Sprinkle with rosemary and serve immediately.

For penne with beet & pumpkin, roast the vegetables as above for 20–25 minutes, omitting the fennel seeds. Cook 11½ oz penne pasta in salted boiling water and drain, reserving one ladleful of the cooking water. Return the pasta to the pan and add the roasted vegetables, a handful of torn basil leaves, and the cooking water. Omit the goat cheese and rosemary. Place over a high heat, stirring, for 30 seconds and serve.

smoked tofu & apricot sausages

Calories per serving **232**
Serves **4**
Preparation time **20 minutes**
Cooking time **10 minutes**

7½ oz **smoked tofu**
2 tablespoons **olive oil** or
  vegetable oil, plus a little
  extra for frying
1 large **onion**, roughly
  chopped
2 **celery sticks**, roughly
  chopped
generous ½ cup roughly
  chopped **no-soak dried
  apricots**
1 cup fresh **bread crumbs**
1 **egg**
1 tablespoon chopped **sage**
salt and **black pepper**

Pat the tofu dry on paper towels and tear into chunks. Heat the oil in a skillet and fry the onion and celery for 5 minutes, until softened. Put them into a food processor and add the tofu and apricots. Blend the ingredients to a chunky paste, scraping down the mixture from the sides of the bowl if necessary.

Put the mixture into a mixing bowl and add the bread crumbs, egg, and sage. Season with salt and pepper and beat well until everything is evenly combined.

Divide the mixture into eight portions. Using lightly floured hands, shape each portion into a sausage, pressing the mixture together firmly.

Heat a little oil in a nonstick skillet and fry the sausages for about 5 minutes, until they are golden. Serve with chunky chips and a spicy relish.

For a spicy apple relish, to serve with the sausages, peel and core 4 cooking apples and cut them into chunks. Place in a saucepan with scant ½ cup dry hard cider, 1 cinnamon stick, 2 teaspoons light brown sugar and ½ teaspoon crushed chiles. Cover and cook over a low heat until the apples have broken up into a pulp. Let cool before serving.

wild mushroom stroganoff

Calories per serving **206**
Serves **4**
Preparation time **15 minutes**
Cooking time **15–16 minutes**

2 tablespoons **butter**
1 tablespoon **olive oil**
1 **onion**, sliced
13 oz **cremini mushrooms**,
   sliced
2 **garlic cloves**, finely
   chopped
2 teaspoons **paprika**, plus
   extra to garnish
6 tablespoons **vodka**
1⅔ cups **Vegetable Stock**
   (see page 44)
generous pinch of **ground
   cinnamon**
generous pinch of **ground
   mace**
5 oz **wild mushrooms**, large
   ones sliced
6 tablespoons **crème fraîche**
   or sour cream
salt and **black pepper**
chopped **parsley**, to garnish

Heat the butter and oil in a skillet, add the onion, and fry for 5 minutes, until lightly browned. Stir in the cup cremini mushrooms and garlic and cook for 4 minutes. Stir in the paprika and cook for 1 minute.

Pour in the vodka. When it is bubbling, flame with a match and stand well back. Once the flames have subsided, stir in the stock, cinnamon, and mace and season with salt and pepper. Simmer for 3–4 minutes.

Add the wild mushrooms and cook for 2 minutes. Stir in 2 tablespoons of the crème fraîche.

Spoon the stroganoff onto serving plates and top with spoonfuls of the remaining crème fraîche, a sprinkling of paprika, and a little parsley. Serve with sweet potato mash.

For sweet potato mash, to serve with the stroganoff, peel 2 large sweet potatoes and cut them into chunks. Steam or boil until tender, then mash with 2 tablespoons crème fraîche and a good grinding of nutmeg. Season with salt and pepper.

chermoula tofu & roasted veg

Calories per serving **241**
Serves **4**
Preparation time **15 minutes**
Cooking time **1 hour**

1 ½ cups finely chopped
  cilantro
3 **garlic cloves**, chopped
1 teaspoon **cumin seeds**,
  lightly crushed
finely grated rind of 1 **lemon**
½ teaspoon **dried crushed**
  chiles
¼ cup **olive oil**
8 oz **tofu**
2 **red onions**, quartered
2 **zucchini**, thickly sliced
2 **red bell peppers**, seeded
  and sliced
2 **yellow bell peppers**,
  seeded and sliced
1 small **eggplant**, thickly
  sliced
salt

Mix the cilantro, garlic, cumin, lemon rind, and chiles together with 1 tablespoon of the oil and a little salt in a small bowl to make the chermoula.

Pat the tofu dry on paper towels and cut it in half. Cut each half horizontally into thin slices. Spread the chermoula generously over the slices.

Scatter the vegetables in a roasting pan and drizzle with the remaining oil. Bake in a preheated oven, 400°F, for about 45 minutes, until lightly browned, turning the ingredients once or twice during cooking.

Arrange the tofu slices over the vegetables, with the side spread with the chermoula uppermost, and bake for another 10–15 minutes, until the tofu is lightly colored. Serve with lightly buttered new potatoes.

For chermoula tuna with tomato & eggplant, omit the tofu, zucchini and bell peppers. Prepare the chermoula as above and rub it all over 4 tuna steaks, about 4 oz each. Set aside to marinate while you cook the vegetables. Scatter the onions in a roasting pan with 2 large eggplants, thickly sliced, and a 13 oz can chopped tomatoes. Stir in the remaining oil and cook for 45 minutes, as above. Heat a large nonstick skillet or grill pan over a high heat and cook the tuna for 1 ½ minutes on each side. Serve with the vegetables.

desserts

strawberry roulade

Calories per serving **110**
Serves **8**
Preparation time **30 minutes**,
  plus cooling
Cooking time **8 minutes**

3 **eggs**
½ cup **superfine sugar**
1 cup **all-purpose flour**
1 tablespoon **hot water**
1 lb fresh or frozen, thawed,
  drained and quartered
  strawberries, or 14 oz can
  **strawberries in natural
  juice**, drained and quartered
¾ cup **plain yogurt**
confectioners' sugar, for
  dusting

Lightly grease a 13 x 9 inch jelly roll pan. Line with a single sheet of wax paper to come about ½ inch above the sides of the pan. Lightly grease the paper.

Whisk the eggs and sugar in a large bowl over a saucepan of hot water until pale and thick. Sift the flour and fold into the egg mixture with the measured hot water. Pour the batter into the prepared pan and bake in a preheated oven, 425°F, for 8 minutes, until golden and set.

Meanwhile, place a sheet of wax paper 1 inch larger all round than the jelly roll pan on a clean damp dish towel. Once cooked, turn out the jelly roll immediately face down on to this second sheet of wax paper. Carefully peel off the lining paper. Roll the sponge up tightly with the new wax paper inside. Wrap the dish towel around the outside and place on a wire rack until cool, then unroll carefully.

Add half the strawberries to the yogurt and spread over the sponge. Roll the sponge up again and trim the ends. Dust with confectioners' sugar and decorate with a few strawberries. Puree the remaining strawberries in a food processor or blender and serve as a sauce with the roll.

For vanilla & jam roll, make the batter as above, folding in ½ teaspoon vanilla extract before baking. Bake, then roll, wrap, and cool as above. Lightly heat ¼ cup raspberry jam and spread it over the sponge. Roll the sponge up again, trim the ends, and dust with confectioners' sugar.

perfect pecan pies

Calories per half pie **303**
Makes **8**
Preparation time **15 minutes**,
  plus chilling and cooling
Cooking time **20 minutes**

½ cup **brown rice flour**
⅓ cup **chickpea flour**
½ cup **cornmeal**
1 teaspoon **xanthan gum**
8 tablespoons **butter**, cubed
2 tablespoons **superfine
  sugar**
1 **egg**, beaten

Filling
½ cup packed **light brown
  sugar**
scant ⅔ cup **butter**
⅓ cup **honey**
1¾ cup **pecan halves**, half of
  them roughly chopped
2 **eggs**, beaten

Place the flours, polenta, xanthan gum, and butter in a food processor and blend until the mixture resembles fine bread crumbs, or rub in by hand in a large bowl. Stir in the sugar.

Add the egg and very gently mix in using a knife, adding enough cold water (probably a couple of teaspoons) to make a dough. Try not to let it become too wet. Knead for a couple of minutes, then wrap closely in plastic wrap and chill for about an hour.

Meanwhile, place the sugar, butter, and honey for the filling in a medium saucepan and heat until the sugar has dissolved. Let stand to cool for 10 minutes.

Remove the dough from the refrigerator while the filling is cooking. Knead it on a surface dusted lightly with rice flour to soften it a little. Divide the dough into eight, then roll each piece out to a thickness of ⅛ inch. Use to line eight individual 4½ inch pie pans, rolling the rolling pin over the top to cut off the excess dough.

Stir the chopped pecans and eggs into the filling mixture and pour into the pastry-lined pans. Arrange the pecan halves over the top, then place the pans in a preheated oven, 400°F, for 15–20 minutes, until the filling is firm. Remove the pies and let cool. Serve with crème fraîche or equal amounts of sour cream and heavy cream mixed together.

caramel pear & marzipan tart

Calories per serving **268**
Serves **8**
Preparation time **10 minutes**,
 plus cooling
Cooking time **45 minutes**

4 tablespoons **unsalted
 butter**
¼ cup packed **light brown
 sugar**
6 ripe **pears**, peeled, halved
 and cored
2 tablespoons **marzipan**
8 oz **store-bought flaky pie
 dough**

Place the butter and sugar in a 9 inch, round cake pan. Place over a moderate heat and cook, stirring continuously, for about 5 minutes, until golden.

Stuff a little marzipan into the cavity of each pear half, then carefully arrange them cut-side up in the pan.

Roll out the pastry on a lightly floured surface to the size of the pan, then place over the top of the pears and press down all around them. Bake in a preheated oven, 375°F, for about 40 minutes, until the pastry is golden and the juices are bubbling.

Cool in the pan for 10 minutes, then invert on to a large plate and serve with a little ice cream.

For pear, blackberry & marzipan tart, roll out the dough as above and place it on a baking sheet. Core and chop 4 pears and combine in a bowl with the light brown sugar, marzipan, and 1 cup blackberries. Omit the butter. Place the fruit in the center of the pastry, leaving a 2 inch rim, then lift the rim up over the edges of the fruit to make a tart. Brush the pastry with 1 tablespoon milk and dust with 1 tablespoon superfine sugar. Bake as above and serve warm.

ricotta, plum, & almond cake

Calories per serving **150**
Serves **6**
Preparation time **30 minutes**,
  plus cooling and chilling
Cooking time **35 minutes**

1 lb **sweet, ripe red plums**,
  quartered and pitted
8 oz **ricotta cheese**
4–5 tablespoons **granulated
  sweetener**
3 **eggs**, separated
¼ teaspoon **almond extract**
¼ cup **slivered almonds**
1 tablespoon **confectioners'
  sugar**, sifted

Arrange half the plums randomly over the bottom of a buttered 8 inch springform pan, the bottom lined with parchment paper.

Mix together the ricotta, 4 tablespoons of the sweetener, the egg yolks, and almond extract in a bowl until smooth.

Whisk the egg whites in a second bowl until stiff, moist peaks form. Fold into the ricotta mixture, then spoon over the plums. Sprinkle the top with the slivered almonds and bake in a preheated oven, 325°F, for 30–35 minutes, until the cake is well risen, golden brown, and the center is just set. Check after 20 minutes and cover the top loosely with foil if the almonds seem to be browning too quickly.

Turn off the oven and let the cake cool for 15 minutes with the door slightly ajar. Cool, then chill well in the refrigerator.

Meanwhile, cook the remaining plums with 2 tablespoons of water in a covered saucepan for 5 minutes, until soft. Puree until smooth, mix in the remaining sweetener, if needed, then pour into a small pitcher.

Remove the pan and lining paper and transfer the cake to a serving plate. Dust the top with the confectioners' sugar and serve, cut into wedges, with the sauce.

chocolate & chestnut roulade

Calories per serving **215**
Serves **8**
Preparation time **15 minutes**,
  plus cooling and chilling
Cooking time **20 minutes**

6 **eggs**, separated
½ cup **superfine sugar**
2 tablespoons **unsweetened cocoa**
1¼ cups **whipping cream**, whipped
generous ⅓ cup **chestnut puree** or **sweetened chestnut spread**
confectioners' sugar, for dusting

Grease and line an 11½ x 7 inch jelly roll pan. Place the egg whites in a large clean bowl and whisk until they form soft peaks. Put the egg yolks and sugar in a separate bowl and whisk together until thick and pale. Fold in the cocoa and the egg whites, then turn into the prepared pan.

Place in a preheated oven, 350°F, for 20 minutes, then remove from the oven and cool in the pan. Turn out on to a piece of wax paper that has been dusted with confectioners' sugar.

Pour the cream into a large clean bowl and whisk until it forms soft peaks. Fold the chestnut puree or spread into the cream, then smooth the mixture over the roulade.

Using the wax paper to help you, carefully roll up the roulade from one short end and lift it gently onto its serving dish (do not worry if it cracks). Dust with confectioners' sugar. Chill until needed and eat on the day it is made.

For chocolate, apricot & walnut roulade, make the cake as above. Whisk the cream for the filling, then fold in 3 tablespoons apricot jam and ½ cup chopped walnuts. Omit the chestnut puree or spread. Spread the filling over the cake and roll the roulade as above. Serve with a dusting of confectioners' sugar.

white chocolate mousse

Calories per serving **192**
Serves **6–8**
Preparation time **10 minutes**,
   plus chilling

7 oz **white chocolate**,
   chopped
¼ cup **milk**
12 **cardamom pods**
7 oz **silken tofu**
¼ cup **superfine sugar**
1 **egg white**
crème fraîche or **plain
   yogurt**, to serve
unsweetened cocoa, for
   dusting

Put the chocolate and milk in a heatproof bowl and melt over a saucepan of gently simmering water. To release the cardamom seeds, crush the pods using a pestle and mortar. Discard the pods and crush the seeds finely.

Place the cardamom seeds and tofu in a food processor with half of the sugar, and blend well to a smooth paste. Turn the mixture into a large bowl.

Whisk the egg white in a thoroughly clean bowl, until it forms peaks. Gradually whisk in the remaining sugar.

Beat the melted chocolate mixture into the tofu until completely combined. Using a large metal spoon, fold in the egg white. Spoon the mousse into small coffee cups or glasses and chill for at least 1 hour. Serve topped with spoonfuls of crème fraîche or yogurt and a light dusting of unsweetened cocoa.

For white chocolate & amaretto pots, make the mousse mixture as above, omitting the cardamom and adding 2 tablespoons amaretto when blending the tofu. Complete the recipe and chill as above. Serve with fresh raspberries instead of the crème fraîche or yogurt and unsweetened cocoa.

chocolate & raspberry soufflés

Calories per serving **287**
Serves **4**
Preparation time **10 minutes**
Cooking time **15 minutes**

3½ oz **bittersweet dark chocolate**
3 **eggs**, separated
generous ⅓ cup **self-rising flour**, sifted
3 tablespoons **superfine sugar**
1¼ cups **raspberries**, plus extra to serve (optional)
confectioners' sugar, for dusting

Break the chocolate into squares and place in a heatproof bowl over a saucepan of simmering water, then let stand until melted.

Place the melted chocolate in a large bowl and whisk in the egg yolks. Fold in the flour.

Whisk the egg whites and superfine sugar in a medium bowl until they form soft peaks. Beat a spoonful of the egg whites into the chocolate mixture to loosen it up before gently folding in the rest.

Divide the raspberries between four lightly greased ramekins, pour over the chocolate mixture, then bake in a preheated oven, 375°F, for 12–15 minutes, until the soufflés have risen.

Dust with confectioners' sugar and serve with extra raspberries, if desired.

For chocolate & coffee soufflés, stir 2 teaspoons instant coffee granules into the hot melted chocolate until it dissolves. Bake the soufflés as above, omitting the raspberries. Make a cappuccino cream to serve with the soufflés by folding 2 tablespoons sweetened strong black coffee into scant ½ cup crème fraîche or plain yogurt. Serve the soufflés straight out of the oven with a dollop of the cream.

brûlée vanilla cheesecake

Calories per serving **160**
Serves **6-8**
Preparation time **30 minutes**,
   plus cooling and chilling
Cooking time **30-35 minutes**

1¾ cups **cream cheese**,
   about 14 oz
6 tablespoons **granulated
   sweetener**
1½ teaspoons **vanilla extract**
finely grated rind of ½ **orange**
4 **eggs**, separated
1 tablespoon **confectioners'
   sugar**, sifted
3 **oranges**, peeled and cut
   into segments, to serve

Mix together the cream cheese, sweetener, vanilla extract, orange rind, and egg yolks in a bowl until smooth.

Whisk the egg whites until softly peaking, then fold a large spoonful into the cheese mixture to loosen it. Add the remaining egg whites and fold them in gently.

Pour the mixture into a buttered, 8 inch springform pan and level the surface. Bake in a preheated oven, 325°F, for 30-35 minutes, until well risen, golden brown, and just set in the center.

Turn off the oven and let the cheesecake cool for 15 minutes with the door slightly ajar. Take it out of the oven, let stand to cool, then chill in the refrigerator for 4 hours. (The cheesecake will sink slightly as it cools.)

Run a knife around the cheesecake, loosen the pan and transfer to a serving plate. Dust the top with the confectioners' sugar and caramelize the sugar with a chef's blowtorch. Serve within 30 minutes, while the sugar topping is still hard and brittle. Cut into wedges and arrange on plates with the orange segments.

orange, rhubarb & ginger slump

Calories per serving **278**
Serves **6**
Preparation time **10 minutes**
Cooking time **20 minutes**

1 ½ lb **rhubarb**, chopped into
   ¾ inch pieces
½ teaspoon **ground ginger**
¼ cup **superfine sugar**
grated rind and juice of
   1 orange
¼ cup **mascarpone cheese**
scant 1 ½ cups **self-rising
   flour**, sifted
4 tablespoons **unsalted
   butter**, cut into small pieces
grated rind of ½ **lemon**
6 tablespoons **milk**

Put the rhubarb, ginger, half the sugar, and orange rind and juice in a medium saucepan. Bring to aboil and simmer gently for 5–6 minutes, until the rhubarb is just tender.

Transfer the rhubarb to an ovenproof dish and spoon over dollops of mascarpone.

Place the flour in a bowl. Add the butter and rub in with the fingertips until the mixture resembles fine bread crumbs. Quickly stir through the remaining sugar, the lemon rind, and milk until combined. Place spoonfuls of the mixture over the rhubarb and mascarpone.

Cook in a preheated oven, 400°F, for 12–15 minutes, until golden and bubbling. Serve with low-fat custard.

For plum & apple slump, replace the rhubarb with 1 lb plums, pitted and cut into ¾ inch pieces, and 1 dessert apple, cored and cubed. Cook with the ginger, sugar and orange until just tender, then transfer to an ovenproof dish. Spoon over ¼ cup crème fraîche or plain yogurt instead of the mascarpone, then complete the recipe as above.

champagne granita

Calories per serving **80**
Serves **6**
Preparation time **25 minutes**,
   plus cooling and freezing

8 tablespoons **sugar**
⅔ cup **boiling water**
scant ¾ cup **medium dry
   champagne**
1 ¼ cups **raspberries**

Stir the sugar into the measured water until it has
dissolved, then let stand to cool.

Mix together the sugar syrup and champagne. Pour it
into a shallow, nonstick baking pan so that it is no more
than 1 inch deep.

Freeze the mixture for 2 hours, until it is mushy,
then break up the ice crystals with a fork. Return the
mixture to the freezer for 2 more hours, beating every
30 minutes, until it has formed fine, icy flakes.

Spoon the granita into elegant glasses and top with
the raspberries.

For pink grapefruit & ginger granita, grate a 1 inch
piece of ginger into the boiling water and sugar
and stir until the sugar has dissolved. Set aside for
30 minutes before mixing the ginger sugar syrup into
1 ¼ cups fresh pink grapefruit juice, instead of the
champagne. Complete the recipe as above, omitting
the raspberries.

rhubarb & ginger parfait

Calories per serving **110**
Serves **6**
Preparation time **20 minutes**,
plus soaking, cooling and
chilling
Cooking time **8–9 minutes**

13 oz **trimmed forced
rhubarb**
1 inch piece of **fresh ginger
root**, peeled and finely
chopped
5 tablespoons **water**
3 teaspoons **powdered
gelatin**
4 **egg yolks**
6 tablespoons **granulated
sweetener**
scant 1 cup **milk**
2 **egg whites**
½ cup **crème fraîche** or **plain
yogurt**
a few drops **pink food
coloring** (optional)
orange rind, to decorate

Slice the rhubarb and put the pieces in a saucepan
with the ginger and 2 tablespoons of the water. Cover
and simmer for 5 minutes, until just tender and still
bright pink. Mash or puree.

Put the remaining water in a small bowl and sprinkle
over the gelatin, making sure that all the powder is
absorbed by the water. Set aside to soak for 5 minutes.

Whisk the egg yolks and sweetener until just mixed.
Pour the milk into a small saucepan and bring just to a
boil. Gradually whisk the milk into the egg yolks, then
pour the mixture back into the saucepan. Slowly bring
the custard almost to the boil, stirring continuously, until
it coats the back of the spoon. Do not let the custard
boil or the eggs will curdle.

Take the pan off the heat and stir in the gelatin until
it has dissolved. Pour into a bowl, stir in the cooked
rhubarb, and let stand to cool.

Whisk the egg whites until stiff, moist peaks form. Fold
the crème fraîche and a few drops of colouring, if used,
into the cooled custard, then fold in the whisked whites.
Spoon into six glasses and chill for 4 hours, until lightly
set. Decorate with orange rind just before serving.

cherry & nectarine pavlova

Calories per serving **245**
Serves **6**
Preparation time **20 minutes**,
  plus cooling
Cooking time **1 hour**

3 **egg whites**
¾ cup **superfine sugar**
1 teaspoon **strong black
  coffee**
1 cup **plain yogurt**
¾ cup **cherries**
scant 1 cup **nectarines**, pitted
  and sliced

Whisk the egg whites in a bowl until they are stiff. Fold in 1 tablespoon of the sugar, then gradually whisk in the remainder. The meringue must be glossy and form peaks when spoonfuls are dropped into the bowl. Fold in the black coffee.

Spread the meringue mixture over a large sheet of parchment paper to form an 8 inch diameter round. Make a slight hollow in the center of the meringue and cook in a preheated oven, 250°F, for 1 hour, until the meringue is crisp. Remove from the oven and let stand to cool on the paper for about 10 minutes before peeling off.

When the meringue is cold, fill the hollow in the top with the yogurt. Arrange the cherries and nectarines chunks on top.

For berry & rose water pavlova, make the meringue mixture as above, folding in ¼ teaspoon rose water before placing it on the baking sheet and baking as above. Combine 8 oz mixed fresh berries (such as strawberries, raspberries, and blueberries) and stir in the rind and juice of ½ lemon. Use instead of the cherries and nectarines as a topping over the yogurt.

tipsy blueberry pots & mascarpone

Calories per serving **175**
Serves **4**
Preparation time **15 minutes**,
  plus soaking and chilling

1 ⅓ cups **blueberries**
2 tablespoons **kirsch** or
  vodka
5 oz **mascarpone cheese**
⅔ cup **plain yogurt**
2 tablespoons **granulated
  sweetener**
grated rind and juice of **1 lime**

Combine 1 cup of the blueberries with the alcohol and let stand to soak for at least 1 hour. Then mash the blueberries.

Beat together the mascarpone and yogurt until smooth, then mix in the sweetener and the lime rind and juice.

Layer alternate spoonfuls of mashed blueberries and mascarpone into individual dishes. Top with the whole blueberries and chill until ready to serve.

For mango pots with ricotta, replace the blueberries with 1 ¼ cups cubed fresh mango and soak in 2 tablespoons vodka. To make the cream, replace the mascarpone with 7 oz ricotta cheese and fold into the yogurt with 2 tablespoons honey, instead of the sugar. Add the lime rind and juice, then assemble the pots as above.

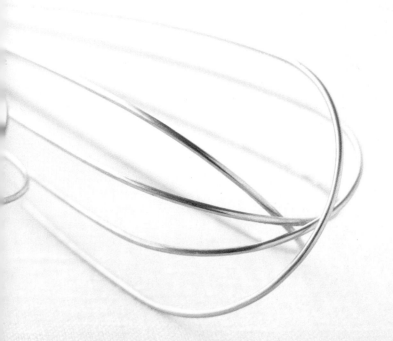

cakes &
bakes

lemon & raspberry cupcakes

Calories per cupcake **206**
Makes **12**
Preparation time **10 minutes**,
  plus cooling
Cooking time **15 minutes**

scant ⅔ cup **butter**, softened
⅔ cup **granulated sugar**
½ cup **rice flour**
½ cup **corn flour**
1 tablespoon **baking powder**
grated rind and juice of
  1 **lemon**
3 **eggs**, beaten
1 cup **raspberries**
1 tablespoon **lemon curd**

Line a large 12-hole muffin pan with large muffin liners. Place all the ingredients except the raspberries and lemon curd in a large bowl and beat together using an electric handheld mixer, or beat with a wooden spoon. Fold in the raspberries.

Spoon half of the mixture into the paper liners, dot over a little lemon curd, then add the remaining sponge mixture.

Place in a preheated oven, 400°F, for 12–15 minutes, until golden and firm to the touch. Remove the cakes from the oven and transfer to a wire rack to cool.

For chocolate & banana cupcakes, make the cupcake batter as above, replacing the raspberries with the chopped flesh of 1 ripe banana. Spoon half the mixture into the paper liners, then top with a small dollop of low-fat chocolate spread instead of the lemon curd. You will need about 1 tablespoon of spread in total. Top with the remaining batter and cook as above.

black currant & almond muffins

Calories per muffin **153**
Makes **12**
Preparation time **5 minutes**,
  plus cooling
Cooking time **25 minutes**

1⅔ cups **all-purpose flour**
2 teaspoons **baking powder**
½ teaspoon **baking soda**
pinch of **salt**
¼ cup **superfine sugar**
a few drops **almond extract**
6 tablespoons **unsalted**
  butter, melted
scant 1 cup **buttermilk**
10 oz can **black currants in**
  natural juice, drained, or
  2¼ cups fresh or frozen
  blackcurrants, defrosted
⅓ cup **slivered almonds**

Sift together the flour, baking powder, baking soda, and salt into a bowl, then stir in the sugar.

Mix together the almond extract, melted butter, buttermilk and black currants in a separate large bowl, then very lightly stir in the dry ingredients. The mixture should still look a little lumpy.

Spoon the mixture into a 12-hole muffin pan lined with muffin liners, sprinkle over the slivered almonds, then bake in a preheated oven, 375°F, for 20–25 minutes, until risen and golden. Carefully lift the liners from the pan and transfer to a wire rack to cool.

For raspberry & coconut muffins, make the muffin batter as above, omitting the almond extract and replacing the black currants with 2 cups fresh raspberries. Spoon into the muffin pan, omit the slivered almonds, and bake. Combine 2 tablespoons dried, unsweetened flaked coconut and 1 teaspoon superfine sugar in a bowl with 1 tablespoon boiling water and set aside while the muffins bake. Spoon the coconut mixture over the muffins when they come out of the oven, then cool on a wire rack.

chocolate mini muffins

Calories per muffin **71**
Makes **40**
Preparation time **30 minutes**,
  plus cooling
Cooking time **15 minutes**

1¼ cups **brown rice flour**
2 tablespoons **chickpea flour**
1 teaspoon **baking soda**
2 teaspoons **baking powder**
½ teaspoon **xanthan gum**
½ cup **superfine sugar**
6 tablespoons **butter**, melted
1 **egg**, beaten
scant 1 cup **buttermilk**
3 oz **milk chocolate drops** or
  milk chocolate, chopped
3 oz **milk chocolate**, to
  decorate

Line four 12-hole mini-muffin pans with 40 paper liners. Sift the flours, baking soda, baking powder, and xanthan gum together into a large bowl, then stir in the sugar.

Mix together the butter, egg, and buttermilk in a separate bowl. Gently combine the dry and wet ingredients, and lightly fold the chocolate drops into the mixture, stirring well.

Spoon the mixture into the paper liners and place in a preheated oven, 400°F, for 15 minutes, until golden and risen. Remove the cakes from the oven and transfer to a wire rack to cool.

Melt the rest of the milk chocolate and drizzle over the cooled muffins before serving.

For chocolate & orange mini muffins, make the muffin batter as above, replacing the milk chocolate with 2 tablespoons unsweetened cocoa. Roughly chop ½ cup candied orange peel and fold into the mixture before baking as above.

banana-toffee bites

Calories per bite **122**
Makes **24**
Preparation time **10 minutes**,
   plus cooling
Cooking time **12 minutes**

1¼ cups **brown rice flour**
6 tablespoons, softened
⅓ cup **superfine sugar**
2 teaspoons **baking powder**
1 large **banana**, mashed
2 **eggs**
6 **toffees**, chopped

Topping
1 tablespoon **light brown
   sugar**
2 tablespoons **chewy banana
   slices** or **dried banana
   chips**

Line two 12-hole mini muffin tins with paper liners. Place all the cake ingredients except the toffees in a food processor and blend until smooth, or beat in a large bowl. Then stir in the toffees.

Spoon the mixture into the paper liners, sprinkle over most of the brown sugar, and place in a preheated oven, 400°F, for 10–12 minutes, until golden and just firm to the touch. Remove the cakes from the oven and cool on a wire rack.

Top with chewy banana slices or banana chips and sprinkle with the remaining sugar.

For butterfly banana & walnut mini muffins, make the muffin mixture as above, replacing the toffees with ½ cup roughly chopped walnuts. Bake as above, then push 2 banana chip halves into each muffin to look like butterfly wings. Serve with a light dusting of confectioners' sugar instead of the brown sugar.

scrumptious strawberry scones

Calories per scone **292**
Makes **8**
Preparation time **10 minutes**,
  plus cooling
Cooking time **12 minutes**

1 cup **rice flour**, plus a little
  extra for dusting
⅔ cup **potato flour**
1 teaspoon **xanthan gum**
1 teaspoon **baking powder**
1 teaspoon **baking soda**
6 tablespoons **butter**, cubed
3 tablespoons **superfine
  sugar**
1 large **egg**, beaten
3 tablespoons **buttermilk**,
  plus a little extra for brushing
⅔ cup **whipping cream**
¾ pint **strawberries**, lightly
  crushed

Place the flours, xanthan gum, baking powder, baking soda, and butter in a food processor and blend until the mixture resembles fine bread crumbs, or rub in by hand in a large bowl. Stir in the sugar. Using the blade of a knife, stir in the egg and buttermilk until the mixture comes together.

Turn the dough out on to a surface dusted lightly with rice flour and gently press it down to a thickness of 1 inch. Using a 2 inch cutter, cut out eight scones. Place on a lightly floured baking sheet, brush with a little buttermilk, then place in a preheated oven, 425°F, for about 12 minutes, until golden and risen. Remove the scones from the oven and transfer to a wire rack to cool.

Meanwhile, whisk the cream until it forms fairly firm peaks and fold the strawberries into it. Slice the scones in half and fill with the strawberry cream.

For raisin scones with black currant cream, make the scones as above, adding ⅓ cup raisins to the raw mixture before shaping. Bake and cool as above. Omit the cream and strawberries. Fold 3 tablespoons black currant compote into ⅔ cup natural fromage frais and use to fill the scones.

fruity mango granola bar

Calories per bar **219**
Makes **12**
Preparation time **10 minutes**,
  plus cooling
Cooking time **30 minutes**

½ cup packed **light brown
  sugar**
scant ⅔ cup **butter**
2 tablespoons **corn syrup**
1 cup **millet flakes**
2 tablespoons **mixed seeds**,
  such as pumpkin and
  sunflower
½ cup roughly chopped **dried
  mango**

Place the sugar, butter, and syrup in a heavy saucepan and heat until melted, then stir in the remaining ingredients.

Spoon the mixture into an 11 x 7 inch nonstick baking pan, press down lightly, and place in a preheated oven, 300°F, for 30 minutes.

Mark into 12 pieces, then cool before removing from the pan. Cut or break into 12 pieces once cooled.

For honey & ginger granola bars, place ¼ cup packed light brown sugar in a pan with 2 tablespoons honey and the butter. Omit the corn syrup. Heat until melted, then add the millet flakes or 1¼ cups rolled oats and the seeds. Instead of the dried mango, stir in 1 ball of preserved ginger, finely chopped. Spoon the mixture into the pan and complete the recipe as above.

apricot, fig & mixed-seed bites

Calories per bite **107**
Makes **24**
Preparation time **10 minutes**,
  plus cooling
Cooking time **15 minutes**

⅔ cup **polyunsaturated margarine**
⅓ cup **light brown sugar**
1 **egg**, beaten
2 tablespoons **water**
⅔ cup **all-purpose wholewheat flour**
½ teaspoon **baking soda**
⅔ cup **rolled oats**
¼ cup chopped **ready-to-eat dried apricots**
¼ cup chopped **dried figs**
⅓ cup **mixed seeds**, such as pumpkin, sunflower, and sesame

Beat together the margarine and sugar in a bowl until light and fluffy, then beat in the egg and measured water.

Sift together the flour and baking soda into the bowl, adding any bran in the sifter. Add the oats, apricots, figs, and seeds, then fold all the ingredients into the margarine and sugar mixture.

Place walnut-size pieces of the mixture on baking sheets lined with wax paper or parchment paper and flatten them slightly with the back of a fork.

Bake in a preheated oven, 350°F, for 10–15 minutes, until golden. Transfer to a wire rack to cool.

For citrus fig & pine nut bites, beat together the margarine and sugar, then beat in the egg and 2 tablespoons orange juice instead of the water. Combine the remaining ingredients in a bowl, as above, replacing the apricots with ½ cup chopped citrus peel, and the mixed seeds with ⅓ cup pine nuts. Shape and cook as above.

mini orange shortbreads

Calories per shortbread **30**
Makes **about 80**
Preparation time **10 minutes**,
  plus cooling
Cooking time **12 minutes**

2 cups **all-purpose flour**,
  sifted
1½ cups **unsalted butter**, cut
  into small pieces
grated rind of 1 **orange**
½ teaspoon **all-spice**
⅓ cup **superfine sugar**
2 teaspoons **cold water**

To serve
2 teaspoons **confectioners'**
  sugar
1 teaspoon **unsweetened**
  cocoa

Place the flour in a bowl, add the butter, and rub in with the fingertips until the mixture resembles fine bread crumbs. Stir in the remaining ingredients with the measured water and mix to form a dough.

Roll out on a lightly floured surface to a thickness of ⅛ inch. Using a ¾ inch plain cutter, cut out approximately 80 rounds.

Place the rounds on nonstick baking sheets and bake in a preheated oven, 400°F, for 10–12 minutes, until golden. Carefully transfer to a wire rack to cool.

Mix together the confectioners' sugar and cocoa and dust a little over the shortbreads before serving.

For cardamom & rose water mini shortbreads, crush 5 cardamom pods and pick out the seeds. Discard the pods. Grind the seeds in a pestle and mortar and place in a bowl with the flour and butter. Rub together the flour and butter as above, then add the orange, sugar, 1½ teaspoons cold water, and ½ teaspoon rose water, omitting the all-spice. Bring the dough together, then roll out and bake as above. Serve dusted in confectioners' sugar, omitting the unsweetened cocoa.

cranberry & hazelnut cookies

Calories per cookie **60**
Makes **30**
Preparation time **10 minutes**,
   plus cooling
Cooking time **6 minutes**

4 tablespoons **unsalted butter**, softened, or **polyunsaturated margarine**
3 tablespoons **granulated sugar**
3 tablespoons **soft light brown sugar**
1 **egg**, beaten
a few drops **vanilla extract**
1¼ cups **self-rising flour**, sifted
⅓ cup **rolled oats**
⅓ cup **dried cranberries**
⅓ cup toasted and chopped **hazelnuts**

Beat together the butter, sugars, egg, and vanilla extract in a large bowl until smooth.

Stir in the flour and oats, then the dried cranberries and chopped hazelnuts.

Place teaspoonfuls of the mixture onto baking sheets lined with wax paper or parchment paper and flatten them slightly with the back of a fork.

Bake in a preheated oven, 350°F, for about 5–6 minutes, until browned. Transfer to a wire rack to cool.

For bittersweet chocolate and ginger cookies, prepare the mixture as above, omitting the cranberries and hazelnuts. Replace them with ¼ cup bittersweet chocolate drops and 2 pieces of chopped preserved ginger or ½ teaspoon of grated fresh ginger root. Stir together and bake as above.

white chocolate drops

Calories per cookie **98**
Makes **20**
Preparation time **10 minutes**,
  plus chilling and cooling
Cooking time **20 minutes**

¼ cup **white vegetable fat**
4 tablespoons **butter**
¼ cup **superfine sugar**
1 **egg yolk**
1¼ cups **brown rice flour**
1 tablespoon **ground
  almonds**
2 oz **white chocolate**, grated
2 teaspoons **confectioners'
  sugar**, to serve

Place the fats and sugar in a large bowl and beat together, then beat in the egg yolk followed by the remaining ingredients. Form the dough into a ball, wrap closely in plastic wrap, and chill for 1 hour.

Remove the dough from the refrigerator, unwrap, and place on a surface dusted lightly with flour. Knead the dough a little to soften it, then divide into 20 balls.

Place the balls on two baking sheets, flatten them slightly with a fork, and place in a preheated oven, 350°F, for about 20 minutes, until golden. Remove the cookies from the oven and transfer to a wire rack to cool. Dust over a little confectioners' sugar before serving.

For chocolate & coconut bites, make the cookies as above, omitting the ground almonds. Melt 2 oz bittersweet chocolate in a bowl over a pan of simmering water. Dip ¼ of each cooled cookie in the chocolate, then dip the chocolate-coated edge of the cookies in ½ cup unsweetened dried, shredded coconut. Place on a tray in the refrigerator for 20 minutes to let the chocolate set, then move the cookies to an airtight container. There will be plenty of leftover chocolate and coconut, but you will need this quantity so that the job of dipping the cookies is not too fussy.

orange & cornmeal cookies

Calories per cookie **67**
Makes **20**
Preparation time **10 minutes**,
   plus chilling and cooling
Cooking time **8 minutes**

½ cup **cornmeal**
2½ tablespoons **rice flour**
¼ cup **ground almonds**
½ teaspoon **baking powder**
⅔ cup **confectioners' sugar**
4 tablespoons **butter**, cubed
1 **egg yolk**, beaten
grated rind 1 **orange**
¼ cup **slivered almonds**

Cover two baking sheets with parchment paper. Place the cornmeal, flour, ground almonds, baking powder, confectioners' sugar, and butter in a food processor and blen until the mixture resembles fine bread crumbs, or rub in by hand in a large bowl.

Stir in the egg yolk and orange rind and bring together to make a dough. Wrap closely in plastic wrap and chill for 30 minutes.

Remove the dough from the refrigerator and roll out thinly on a surface dusted lightly with flour. Cut into 20 rounds with a 1½ inch cutter. Transfer to the prepared baking sheets, sprinkle with the almonds, and place in a preheated oven, 350°F, for about 8 minutes, until golden. Remove the cookies from the oven, let stand for a few minutes to harden, then transfer to a wire rack to cool.

For Christmasy cornmeal cookies, prepare the dough as above, adding ¼ teaspoon vanilla extract and ½ teaspoon each ground cinnamon and all-spice when stirring in the egg. Chill and roll out as above, then use star-shape cookie cutters of different sizes to cut out the cookies. Place on baking sheets lined with parchment paper and cook as above, omitting the slivered almonds.

lemon, pistachio & date squares

Calories per square **174**
Makes **15–20**
Preparation time **10 minutes**,
  plus cooling and chilling
Cooking time **20 minutes**

grated rind of **1 lemon**
scant ½ cup chopped **ready-
  to-eat dried dates**
½ cup chopped **unsalted
  pistachios**
¾ cup chopped, **slivered
  almonds**
generous ½ cup packed **light
  brown sugar**
¾ cup **millet flakes**
1½ cups **cornflakes**, lightly
  crushed
13 oz can **condensed milk**
1 oz **mixed seeds**, such as
  pumpkin and sunflower

Simply place all the ingredients in a large bowl and mix together. Spoon into an 11 x 7 inch baking pan and place in a preheated oven, 350°F, for 20 minutes.

Remove from the oven, let stand to cool, then mark into 15–20 squares and chill until firm. If you want, you could drizzle the top with some melted chocolate once the squares are cooled.

For chocolate & almond squares, make the mixture as above, omitting the pistachios and slivered almonds. Roughly chop ⅔ cup blanched almonds and add to the mixture with 1⅔ cups bran flakes and 2 oz melted bittersweet chocolate. Cook and cool, mark and chill as above, drizzling the top with melted white chocolate once cooled, if liked.

passion cake squares

Calories per square **307**
Makes **16**
Preparation time **10 minutes**,
  plus cooling
Cooking time **1 hour**

1 cup **brown rice flour**
1⅔ cups **superfine sugar**
2 teaspoons **baking powder**
1 teaspoon **xanthan gum**
1 teaspoon **ground cinnamon**
⅔ cup **canola** or **corn oil**
2 **eggs**, beaten
a few drops **vanilla extract**
⅔ cup grated **carrots**
½ cup **dried, unsweetened
  shredded coconut**
3½ oz **canned crushed
  pineapple**, drained
⅓ cup **golden raisins**

Topping
scant 1 cup **cream cheese**
2 tablespoons **runny honey**
⅔ cup chopped **walnuts**
  (optional)

Grease and flour an 8 inch square cake pan. Sift together the flour, sugar, baking powder, xanthan gum, and cinnamon into a large bowl. Add the oil, eggs, and vanilla extract and beat well.

Fold in the carrots, coconut, pineapple, and golden raisins and spoon the mixture into the prepared pan. Place in a preheated oven, 350°F, for about 1 hour, or until a skewer inserted in the middle comes out clean. Remove from the oven and cool in the pan.

Beat together the cream cheese and honey and smooth over the cake, then sprinkle the nuts, if using, on top. Cut into 16 squares.

For tropical cake squares, prepare the cake batter as in the first step above, omitting the cinnamon. Peel and pit 1 small ripe mango and roughly chop it. Fold it into the batter with the carrots, coconut, and ⅓ cup chopped Brazil nuts. Omit the pineapple and golden raisins. Bake and cool as above. For the topping, fold the flesh of 3 passion fruits into the cream cheese, sweeten with honey to taste, then spread over the cake. Cut into squares, omitting the walnuts.

moist banana & carrot cake

Calories per serving **183**

Serves **14**

Preparation time **10 minutes**, plus cooling

Cooking time **1 hour 40 minutes**

1 cup **dried apricots**, roughly chopped

½ cup **water**

1 **egg**

2 tablespoons **honey**

1 cup roughly chopped **walnuts**

1 lb ripe **bananas**, mashed

1 large **carrot**, about 4 oz, grated

1¾ cups **self-rising flour**, sifted

Topping

⅔ cup **cream cheese**

2 tablespoons **lemon curd**

Place the apricots in a small saucepan with the measured water, bring to a boil, and simmer for 10 minutes. Transfer to a liquidizer or food processor and blend to create a thick puree.

Put all the other cake ingredients in a large bowl and add the apricot puree. Mix well, then spoon into a greased and lined 9 x 5 x 3 inch loaf pan.

Bake in a preheated oven, 350°F, for 1½ hours, or until a skewer inserted in the middle comes out clean. Turn out onto a wire rack to cool.

Beat together the cream cheese and lemon curd and spread over the top of the loaf.

For a date & banana cake, replace the apricots with generous ¾ cup dates. Cook and puree as above, reducing the water to ⅓ cup. Make the cake batter with all the above ingredients, using the date puree instead of the apricot and adding 2 teaspoons all-spice. Cook and let cool as above. Combine 1 teaspoon ground cinnamon with 2 tablespoons superfine sugar and dust over the cake, instead of the lemon topping.

lemon drizzle loaf

Calories per serving **334**
Serves **12**
Preparation time **10 minutes**
Cooking time **40 minutes**

1 cup **butter**, softened
generous 1 cup **superfine sugar**
1½ cups **brown rice flour**
2 teaspoons **baking powder**
4 **eggs**, beaten
grated rind and juice of
  1 **lemon**

Lemon drizzle
grated rind and juice of
  2 **lemons**
scant ½ cup **superfine sugar**

Grease and line a 9 x 5 x 3 inch loaf pan. Place all the cake ingredients in a food processor and blend until smooth, or beat in a large bowl.

Pour the mixture into the prepared pan and place in a preheated oven, 350°F, for 35–40 minutes, until golden and firm to the touch. Remove the cake from the oven and transfer to a wire rack.

Prick holes all over the sponge with a toothpick. Place the drizzle ingredients in a bowl and mix together, then drizzle the liquid over the warm loaf. Let stand until completely cold. Decorate with a twist of lemon rind, if desired.

For citrus cranberry loaf, make the cake batter as above, replacing the brown rice flour with regular white rice flour and using the rind and juice of ½ orange, instead of the lemon. Fold in generous ¾ cup dried cranberries and bake as above. Make the lemon drizzle, adding 1 tablespoon brandy to the mix, and use as above.

chocolate, zucchini & nut cake

Calories per serving **266**
Serves **12**
Preparation time **10 minutes**,
  plus cooling
Cooking time **40 minutes**

1 medium **zucchini**, about
  8 oz, coarsely grated
2 **eggs**
scant ½ cup **vegetable oil**
grated rind and juice of
  1 **orange**
½ cup **superfine sugar**
1¾ cups **self-rising flour**
2 tablespoons **unsweetened
  cocoa**
½ teaspoon **baking soda**
½ teaspoon **baking powder**
¼ cup **dried apricots**,
  chopped

Topping
scant 1 cup **cream cheese**
2 tablespoons **chocolate
  hazelnut spread**
1 tablespoon **hazelnuts**,
  toasted and chopped

Place the zucchini in a strainer and squeeze out any excess liquid.

Beat together the eggs, oil, orange rind and juice, and sugar in a large bowl. Sift in the flour, unsweetened cocoa, baking soda and baking powder and beat to combine.

Fold in the zucchini and apricots, then spoon the mixture into a greased and lined 8 inch deep springform cake pan.

Bake in a preheated oven, 350°F, for 40 minutes, until risen and firm to the touch. Turn out onto a wire rack to cool.

Beat together the cream cheese and chocolate hazelnut spread and spread over the top of the cake. Sprinkle over the hazelnuts.

For a strawberry & yogurt topping, to use instead of the chocolate and hazelnut topping, blend ⅔ cup strawberries in a blender or food processor with 1 tablespoon honey to make a puree. Stir in ½ cup plain yogurt and spread over the top of the cooled cake. Decorate the top of the cake with halved strawberries, if liked.

potato & thyme griddle cakes

Calories per scone **91**
Makes **6**
Preparation time **10 minutes**
Cooking time **5 minutes**

1 medium **potato**, abput 8 oz,
  chopped into 2 cm (¾ inch)
  cubes and cooked in boiling
  water for 10 minutes
⅓ cup **rice flour**
pinch of **salt**
1 teaspoon **baking powder**
1 teaspoon fresh **thyme**,
  chopped
2 tablespoons **buttermilk**
1 **egg**, beaten
a little **oil** and **butter**, for
  cooking

Place the potatoes and a pat of butter in a large
bowl and mash together until smooth, then stir in the
remaining ingredients until combined. Bring the mixture
together to form a ball.

Turn out onto a surface dusted lightly with flour,
roll into a round about ¼ inch thick, and cut into
six triangles.

Brush a grill pan or nonstick skillet with a little oil and
add a pat of butter, then cook the griddle cakes for a
few minutes on each side until golden. Serve with
butter and cheese.

**For saffron potato griddle cakes with herbed
cream cheese**, soak a large pinch of saffron strands
in 1 tablespoon hot water for 15 minutes. Meanwhile
cook and mash the potatoes as above. Mix the
saffron-infused water and the remaining ingredients,
omitting the thyme. Shape and cook as above. Stir
2 tablespoons each chopped basil and chopped
parsley into ⅔ cup cream cheese and serve with the
warm griddle cakes.

garlic & caramelized onion bhajis

Calories per bhaji **310**
Makes **6**
Preparation time **20 minutes**
Cooking time **5 minutes**

2 tablespoons **olive oil**
1 **onion**, sliced
2 **garlic cloves**, sliced
1 teaspoon **cumin seeds**
2 tablespoons chopped
  cilantro
1⅓ cups **chickpea flour**
1 teaspoon **baking soda**
½ teaspoon **salt**
1 cup **water**

Heat half the oil in a nonstick skillet, add the onion, garlic, and cumin and fry for 5–6 minutes, until golden and softened. Stir through the cilantro.

Meanwhile, mix together the flour, baking soda, salt, and measured water in a bowl and set aside for 10 minutes, then stir it into the onion mixture.

Heat a little of the remaining oil in the skillet and add spoonfuls of the mix, frying for 2–3 minutes, turning halfway through cooking. Cook the remaining mix in the same way.

For a herb & yogurt chutney, to serve with the bhajis, blend 2 tablespoons yogurt, a handful of mint leaves, and a handful of cilantro leaves in a blender or food processor with 1 tablespoon lemon juice, until smooth. Stir into a bowl with another ¼ cup plain yogurt and season with salt. Cover and keep chilled until ready to serve the bhajis.

feta & herb loaf

Calories per serving **118**
Serves **14**
Preparation time **10 minutes**,
  plus rising and cooling
Cooking time **45 minutes**

1 ⅓ cups **cornmeal**
⅔ cup **rice flour**
¾ cup **dried milk powder**
pinch of **salt**
¼ oz envelope **easy-blend dry
  yeast**
2 teaspoons **superfine sugar**
2 teaspoons **xanthan gum**
3 **eggs**, beaten
2 tablespoons chopped
  mixed herbs
scant 2 cups **tepid water**
3½ oz **feta cheese**, crumbled

Grease and line a 9 x 5 x 3 inch loaf pan. Sift the cornmeal, flour, milk powder, and salt into a large bowl and stir well to combine. Stir in the yeast, sugar, and xanthan gum.

Place the eggs, herbs, and measured water in a bowl and mix together. Stir this mixture into the dry ingredients and combine to form a soft dough. Beat for 5 minutes, then stir in the feta cheese.

Spoon the mixture into the prepared pan, cover with a clean damp dish towel, and let stand in a warm place to rise for about 30 minutes, until the mixture is near the top of the pan. Place in a preheated oven, 350°F, for about 45 minutes, until brown and hollow-sounding when tapped.

Remove the loaf from the oven and transfer to a wire rack to cool.

For cornmeal, spinach & chile loaf, make the dough as above, replacing the feta cheese with ½ cup cooked spinach (squeezed dry in a dish towel, then finely chopped), 1 teaspoon caraway seeds, and 1 seeded and finely chopped red chile. Let stand to rise in the pan, bake, and cool as above.

nutty seed loaf

Calories per serving **263**
Serves **8**
Preparation time **10 minutes**,
  plus cooling
Cooking time **25 minutes**

2½ cups **brown rice flour**
¼ cup **rice bran**
2 tablespoons **dry milk
  powder**
½ teaspoon **baking soda**
1 teaspoon **baking powder**
½–1 teaspoon **salt**
1 teaspoon **xanthan gum**
pinch of **superfine sugar**
⅓ cup **mixed seeds**, such as
  sunflower and pumpkin
½ cup toasted and roughly
  chopped **hazelnuts**
1 **egg**, lightly beaten
1¼ cups **buttermilk**

Place all the dry ingredients, including the nuts, in a large bowl and mix together. In a separate bowl, mix together the egg and buttermilk, then stir into the dry ingredients.

Turn the dough out on to a surface dusted lightly with flour and form into a round about 8 inches in diameter. Mark into eight segments, then place on a baking sheet and dust with a little extra flour.

Place in an oven preheated to its highest setting and cook for 10 minutes, then reduce the heat to 400°F, and continue to cook for about 15 minutes, until the loaf is golden and sounds hollow when tapped.

Remove the loaf from the oven and transfer to a wire rack to cool.

For seeded Parmesan rolls, make the dough as above, using ⅓ cup sesame seeds instead of the mixed seeds, and replacing the hazelnuts with ½ cup grated Parmesan cheese. Shape the dough into 8 round rolls, then place on a baking sheet and dust with a little extra flour. Bake for 10 minutes as above, then reduce the oven heat as above and cook for an additional 8–10 minutes, until the rolls sound hollow when tapped.

pizza scrolls

Calories per scroll **331**
Makes **8**
Preparation time **25 minutes**,
  plus rising
Cooking time **15 minutes**

two ¼ oz envelopes **quick-
  rising active dry yeast**
1 teaspoon **superfine sugar**
1 cup **milk**, warmed
1 cup **rice flour**
1 cup **potato flour**
1 teaspoon **baking powder**
1 teaspoon **xanthan gum**
pinch of **salt**
1 tablespoon **sunflower oil**
1 **egg**, beaten

Filling
¼ cup **pureed tomatoes**
2 cups grated **mixed cheese**,
  such as mozzarella and
  cheddar
3 oz **wafer-thin ham**,
  shredded
handful of **basil**, chopped

Place the yeast, sugar, and milk in a bowl and set aside for about 10 minutes, until frothy. In a large bowl, stir together the flours, baking powder, xanthan gum and salt.

Mix the oil and egg into the yeast mixture and pour this into the flour mixture, using a fork to bring the mixture together. Turn it out onto a surface dusted lightly with rice flour and knead for 5 minutes, adding a little flour if the mixture becomes sticky. Place in a lightly oiled bowl, cover with a damp cloth, and let stand to rise in a warm place for about 40 minutes, or until well risen.

Roll the dough out on the floured surface into a rectangle approximately 12 x 10 inches. Spread with the pureed tomatoes, then sprinkle over the other fillings. Roll the pizza up from one long edge, then slice into eight pieces.

Arrange the rolled-up pizza scrolls side by side on a lightly oiled heavy baking sheet or pan. They should be pushed up against each other so the sides are touching. Place in a preheated oven, 425°F, for 12–15 minutes, until golden. Eat warm from the oven.

For a large prosciutto & arugula pizza, make the pizza dough and let it rise as above. Roll it out onto a large baking sheet dusted with flour and spread with the pureed tomatoes, then sprinkle over the cheese. Omit the ham. Bake in a preheated oven, 425°F, for 12–15 minutes, until golden. Remove from the heat, drape over 5 slices prosciutto, and scatter with the basil and a handful of arugula leaves. Serve cut into squares.

olive & haloumi bread

Calories per serving **189**
Serves **12**
Preparation time **15 minutes**,
  plus rising and cooling
Cooking time **25 minutes**

4 cups **white bread flour**,
  plus extra for sifting
¼ oz envelope **quick-rising
  active dry yeast**
pinch of **salt**
2 tablespoons **olive oil**
1¼ cups **warm water**
1 **onion**, thinly sliced
⅔ cup **pitted olives**
3 oz **haloumi cheese**,
  chopped
2 tablespoons chopped
  parsley

Place the flour, yeast, and salt in a large bowl. Combine half the oil with the measured water and stir into the flour to form a dough.

Turn the dough out on a lightly floured surface and knead for 5 minutes, until smooth and elastic. Place in a lightly oiled bowl, cover with a damp cloth, and set aside in a warm place for about 1 hour, until doubled in size.

Meanwhile, heat the remaining oil in a skillet, add the onion, and fry for 7–8 minutes, until softened and golden. Let stand to cool.

Turn the risen dough out on the floured surface and add the remaining ingredients, including the onion, kneading it into the dough. Shape into an oval, place on a lightly floured baking sheet, and let stand to rise for 1 hour.

When the loaf has risen, slash a few cuts in the top, sift over a little flour, then bake in a preheated oven, 425°F, for about 25 minutes, until hollow-sounding when tapped. Transfer to a wire rack to cool.

For olive & sundried tomato swirls, make the dough and let stand to rise until doubled in size. Fry the onions in the oil as above, then stir in the olives, ¾ cup sundried tomatoes, and ½ teaspoon fennel seeds, and let stand to cool. Roll the dough out on a floured surface to the size of 8 x 11 inches and spread with the olive, onion, and tomato mix. Roll up the dough from one long end and cut the roll into 12 rounds. Lay them on a large baking sheet dusted with flour, cover with a damp cloth, and let stand to rise for 30 minutes. Bake in a preheated oven, 425°F, for 12–15 minutes, until golden.

index

acknowledgments

Executive Editor: Eleanor Maxfield
Editor: Ruth Wiseall
Creative Director: Tracy Killick
Designer: Geoff Fennell
Photographer: William Shaw
Home Economist: Marina Filippelli
Props Stylist: Liz Hippisley
Senior Production Controller:
    Carolin Stransky

Special photography: © Octopus Publishing Group Limited/William Shaw.
Other photography: © Octopus Publishing Group Limited/Stephen
Conroy 55, 57, 61, 85, 153; /Will Heap 162; /David Munns 42;
/Emma Neish 167, 173, 193, 199, 201, 203, 213, 215, 217, 221,
225, 227, 229, 231, 233; /Lis Parsons 17, 21, 83, 95, 97, 100, 103,
105, 107, 113, 117, 119, 123, 125, 129, 145, 149, 157, 161, 169,
177, 181, 195, 205, 209, 219, 223, 235; /William Reavell 29, 99,
109, 111, 115, 121, 141; /Craig Robertson 25, 33, 35, 47, 89, 93;
/Ian Wallace 6, 14, 126, 190.